Slow Cooking

IN THE SLOW COOKER • ON THE STOVE TOP • IN THE OVEN

NOTE: Please read the
instruction manual for
your electric slow cooker
carefully and follow its
safety guidelines.

The oven temperatures
in this book are for
fan-forced ovens. If you
have a conventional oven,
increase the temperature by
10-20 degrees. The imperial
measurements used in these
recipes are approximate only
and should not affect your
cooking results. A conversion
chart appears on page 197.

CONTENTS

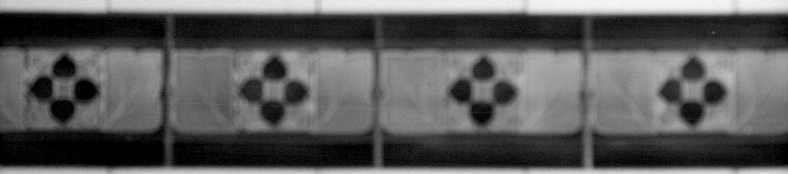

IN THE SLOW COOKER

There's something wonderfully comforting about slow-cooked food. Perhaps it's that sensational aroma that fills your house and the irresistibly rich flavours that warm your soul. Or the melt-in-the mouth texture of slow-cooked meats and the fact that you can create a hearty crowd-pleasing meal without spending much money or time in the kitchen. For whatever reason, slow-cooked food is undeniably delicious and, best of all, it practically cooks itself; this is especially so if you are using a slow cooker. Slow cookers are perfect for this style of cooking. You can throw all the ingredients into the pot in the morning, switch it on and come home in the evening to a welcoming aroma at the door and your dinner ready. Or you can simply have it bubbling away while you get on with other jobs. We used a 4.5-litre (18-cup) slow cooker, the most popular size, for our recipes. If you have a smaller or larger slow cooker you may need to increase or decrease the quantity of food, and almost certainly the liquid content, in the recipes.

SOUP

LAMB SHANK, FENNEL AND VEGETABLE SOUP

serves 6
prep + cook time
10½ hours
nutritional count per serving
6.1g total fat
(1.4g saturated fat);
953kJ (228 cal);
13.6g carbohydrate;
26.3g protein; 6.7g fibre

Suitable to freeze at the end of step 2.

Serve soup with lemon wedges, greek-style yogurt and crusty bread.

1 tablespoon olive oil
4 french-trimmed lamb shanks (1kg)
1 medium brown onion (150g), chopped coarsely
2 baby fennel bulbs (260g), sliced thinly
2 medium carrots (240g), chopped coarsely
4 cloves garlic, crushed
2 fresh small red thai (serrano) chillies, chopped finely
2 teaspoons ground cumin
2 teaspoons ground coriander
1 teaspoon ground cinnamon

1 teaspoon caraway seeds
pinch saffron threads
1.5 litres (6 cups) water
2 cups (500ml) beef stock
400g (14½ ounces) canned diced tomatoes
400g (15 ounces) canned chickpeas (garbanzo beans), rinsed, drained
¾ cup (90g) frozen baby peas
1 cup loosely packed fresh coriander (cilantro) leaves

1   Heat half the oil in large frying pan; cook lamb, until browned all over, then place in 4.5-litre (18-cup) slow cooker.
2   Heat remaining oil in same pan; cook onion, fennel, carrot, garlic and chilli, stirring, until onion softens. Add spices; cook, stirring, until fragrant. Place vegetable mixture into cooker. Stir in the water, stock, undrained tomatoes and chickpeas. Cook, covered, on low, 10 hours.
3   Remove lamb from cooker. When cool enough to handle, remove meat from bones, shred meat; discard bones. Stir meat, peas and coriander leaves into cooker. Season to taste.

Ribollita [ree-boh-lee-tah] literally means 'reboiled'. This famous Tuscan soup was originally made by reheating leftover minestrone or vegetable soup and adding chunks of bread, white beans and other vegetables such as carrot, zucchini, spinach and cavolo nero. Cavolo nero, or tuscan cabbage, is a member of the kale family, if you can't find it use cabbage or silver beet (swiss chard) instead.

RIBOLLITA

1 ham hock (1kg)
1 medium brown onion (150g), chopped finely
2 stalks celery (300g), trimmed, sliced thinly
1 large carrot (180g), chopped finely
1 small fennel bulb (200g), sliced thinly
3 cloves garlic, crushed
400g (14½ ounces) canned diced tomatoes
2 sprigs fresh rosemary
½ teaspoon dried chilli flakes

2 litres (8 cups) water
375g (12 ounces) cavolo nero, shredded coarsely
400g (15 ounces) canned cannellini beans, rinsed, drained
½ cup coarsely chopped fresh basil
250g (½ pound) sourdough bread, crust removed
½ cup (40g) flaked parmesan cheese

serves 6
prep + cook time 8¾ hours
nutritional count per serving
4.9g total fat
(2.1g saturated fat);
798kJ (191 cal);
18g carbohydrate;
15.1g protein; 7g fibre

Suitable to freeze at the end of step 1.

1 Combine hock, onion, celery, carrot, fennel, garlic, undrained tomatoes, rosemary, chilli and the water in 4.5-litre (18-cup) slow cooker. Cook, covered, on low, 8 hours.
2 Remove hock from cooker; add cavolo nero and beans to soup. Cook, covered, on high, about 20 minutes or until cavolo nero is wilted.
3 Meanwhile, when hock is cool enough to handle, remove meat from bone; shred coarsely. Discard skin, fat and bone. Add meat and basil to soup; season to taste.
4 Break chunks of bread into serving bowls; top with soup and cheese.

Black beans, also known as black turtle beans, have long been a staple food in Latin America and South America. They are commonly used in soups and stews, and are an extremely good source of antioxidants. They have a meaty, dense texture and a flavour similar to mushrooms.

CUBAN BLACK BEAN SOUP

serves 6
prep + cook time
8 hours 55 minutes
(+ standing)
nutritional count per serving
18.1g total fat
(2.9g saturated fat);
1350kJ (323 cal);
9.6g carbohydrate;
24.7g protein; 12.4g fibre

Suitable to freeze at the end of step 6.

1½ cups (300g) dried black turtle beans
1 ham hock (1kg)
2 tablespoons olive oil
1 large brown onion (200g), chopped finely
1 medium red capsicum (bell pepper) (200g), chopped finely
3 garlic cloves, crushed
3 teaspoons ground cumin
1 teaspoon dried chilli flakes

400g (14½ ounces) canned crushed tomatoes
2 litres (8 cups) water
3 teaspoons dried oregano leaves
1 teaspoon ground black pepper
2 tablespoons lime juice
1 large tomato (220g), chopped finely
¼ cup coarsely chopped fresh coriander (cilantro)

1 Place beans in medium bowl, cover with cold water; stand overnight.
2 Drain and rinse beans, place in medium saucepan, cover with cold water; bring to the boil. Boil, uncovered, 15 minutes; drain.
3 Meanwhile, preheat oven to 200°C/400°F.
4 Roast ham on oven tray for 30 minutes.
5 Heat oil in large frying pan; cook onion, capsicum and garlic, stirring, until onion is soft. Add cumin and chilli; cook, stirring, until fragrant.
6 Combine beans, ham, onion mixture, undrained tomatoes, the water, oregano and pepper in 4.5-litre (18-cup) slow cooker. Cook, covered, on low, 8 hours.
7 Remove ham from cooker. When cool enough to handle, remove meat from bone; shred coarsely. Discard skin, fat and bone. Cool soup 10 minutes, then blend or process 2 cups soup mixture until smooth. Return meat to cooker with pureed soup, stir in juice and tomato; sprinkle with coriander. Season to taste.

ITALIAN CHICKEN SOUP

serves 6
prep + cook time
9 hours
nutritional count per serving
14.1g total fat
(4.4g saturated fat);
1580kJ (378 cal);
23.2g carbohydrate;
37g protein; 4.5g fibre

Suitable to freeze at the
end of step 2.

1.5kg (3 pound) chicken
3 large tomatoes (650g)
1 medium brown onion (150g),
  chopped coarsely
2 stalks celery (300g), trimmed,
  chopped coarsely
1 large carrot (180g), chopped coarsely
2 bay leaves

4 cloves garlic, peeled, halved
6 black peppercorns
2 litres (8 cups) water
¾ cup (155g) risoni pasta
½ cup coarsely chopped fresh flat-leaf parsley
½ cup coarsely chopped fresh basil
2 tablespoons finely chopped fresh oregano
¼ cup (60ml) fresh lemon juice

1   Discard as much skin as possible from chicken. Chop 1 tomato coarsely; chop remaining tomatoes finely, refrigerate, covered, until required.
2   Place chicken, coarsely chopped tomato, onion, celery, carrot, bay leaves, garlic, peppercorns and the water in 4.5-litre (18-cup) slow cooker. Cook, covered, on low, 8 hours.
3   Carefully remove chicken from cooker. Strain broth through fine sieve into large heatproof bowl; discard solids. Skim and discard any fat from broth. Return broth to cooker; add risoni and finely chopped tomatoes. Cook, covered, on high, about 30 minutes or until risoni is tender.
4   Meanwhile, when cool enough to handle, remove meat from bones; shred coarsely. Discard bones. Add chicken, herbs and juice to soup; cook, covered, on high, 5 minutes. Season to taste.

BORSCHT

60g (2 ounces) butter
2 medium brown onions (300g),
    chopped finely
500g (1 pound) beef chuck steak, cut
    into large chunks
1 cup (250ml) water
750g (1½ pounds) beetroot (beets),
    peeled, chopped finely
2 medium potatoes (400g), chopped finely

2 medium carrots (240g), chopped finely
4 small (360g) finely chopped tomatoes
1 litre (4 cups) beef stock
⅓ cup (80ml) red wine vinegar
3 bay leaves
4 cups (320g) finely shredded cabbage
2 tablespoons coarsely chopped fresh
    flat-leaf parsley
½ cup (120g) sour cream

serves 6
prep + cook time
8 hours 50 minutes
nutritional count per serving
20.6g total fat
(12.4g saturated fat);
1689kJ (404 cal);
25.3g carbohydrate;
25.3g protein; 8.8g fibre

Suitable to freeze at the
end of step 1.

1   Melt half the butter in large frying pan; cook onion, stirring, until soft. Place onion in
4.5-litre (18-cup) slow cooker. Melt remaining butter in same pan; cook beef, stirring,
until browned all over. Place beef in cooker. Add the water to the same pan; bring to the
boil, then add beetroot, potato, carrot, tomato, stock, vinegar and bay leaves to slow cooker.
Cook, covered, on low, 8 hours.
2   Discard bay leaves. Remove beef from soup; shred using two forks. Return beef to soup with
cabbage; cook, covered, on high, about 20 minutes or until cabbage is wilted. Stir in parsley.
3   Serve soup topped with sour cream.

Pumpkin soup is one of those simple, comforting classics that everyone loves. It needs nothing more than a thick slice of warm, buttered bread to dunk in and mop up the creamy pumpkin goodness. You can use any type of pumpkin variety in this soup, but to get that sweet nutty flavour and velvety smooth texture, butternut pumpkin is the best.

PUMPKIN SOUP

30g (1 ounce) butter
1 tablespoon olive oil
1 large leek (500g), sliced thinly
1.8kg (3¾ pounds) piece pumpkin, chopped coarsely
1 large potato (300g), chopped coarsely
3 cups (750ml) chicken stock
3 cups (750ml) water
½ cup (125ml) pouring cream
1 tablespoon finely chopped fresh chives

1   Heat butter and oil in large frying pan; cook leek, stirring, until soft.
2   Combine leek, pumpkin, potato, stock and the water in 4.5-litre (18-cup) slow cooker. Cook, covered, on low, 6 hours.
3   Cool soup 10 minutes. Blend or process soup, in batches, until smooth. Return soup to cooker. Cook, covered, on high, about 20 minutes or until hot. Stir in ⅓ cup of the cream. Season to taste.
4   Serve soup topped with remaining cream and chives.

serves 6
prep + cook time
6½ hours
nutritional count per serving
17.9g total fat
(10.1g saturated fat);
1275kJ (305 cal);
24.8g carbohydrate;
9g protein; 5.1g fibre

Suitable to freeze to at the end of step 2.

PORK AND FENNEL SOUP

serves 6
prep + cook time
6 hours 40 minutes
nutritional count per serving
16.2g total fat
(8.4g saturated fat);
1258kJ (301 cal);
14.9g carbohydrate;
22g protein; 4.3g fibre

Suitable to freeze at the end
of step 1. Thaw and reheat
soup, then shred pork.

Reserve some of the feathery
fennel fronds to sprinkle over
the soup at serving time.

500g (1 pound) piece pork neck
4 small potatoes (500g), chopped coarsely
2 large fennel bulbs (1kg), chopped coarsely
  (see tip)
1 medium brown onion (150g),
  chopped coarsely
2 cloves garlic, quartered

1 bay leaf
6 black peppercorns
1.5 litres (6 cups) water
2 cups (500ml) chicken stock
½ cup (125ml) pouring cream

1 Tie pork at 2.5cm (1 inch) intervals with kitchen string. Combine the pork, potato, fennel, onion, garlic, bay leaf, peppercorns, the water and stock in 4.5-litre (18-cup) slow cooker. Cook, covered, on low, 6 hours.
2 Discard bay leaf. Transfer pork to medium bowl; remove string. Using two forks, shred pork coarsely.
3 Stand soup 10 minutes, then blend or process, in batches, until smooth. Return soup to cooker; stir in cream. Cook, covered, on high, until hot. Season to taste.
4 Serve soup topped with pork and reserved fennel fronds.

PEA AND HAM SOUP

500g (1 pound) green split peas
1 tablespoon olive oil
1 large brown onion (200g), chopped finely
3 cloves garlic, crushed
1 ham hock (1kg)
2 medium carrots (240g), chopped finely

2 stalks celery (300g), trimmed,
  chopped finely
4 fresh thyme sprigs
2 bay leaves
2 litres (8 cups) water

serves 6
prep + cook time
8 hours 20 minutes
nutritional count per serving
6.4g total fat
(1.2g saturated fat);
1517kJ (363 cal);
43g carbohydrate;
27.3g protein; 11g fibre

Suitable to freeze at the
end of step 2.

Serve topped with coarsely
chopped mint leaves, thinly
sliced green onions (scallions)
and greek-style yogurt.

1 Rinse peas under cold water until water runs clear; drain.
2 Heat oil in large frying pan; cook onion and garlic, stirring, until onion softens. Place
onion mixture into 4.5-litre (18-cup) slow cooker; stir in peas and remaining ingredients.
Cook, covered, on low, 8 hours.
3 Remove ham from cooker. When cool enough to handle, remove meat from bone; shred
coarsely, return meat to slow cooker. Discard skin, fat and bone. Season soup to taste.

Don't be fooled by the uninviting exterior of this root vegetable. Once its tough, knobbly outer layer is peeled away, a creamy, smooth white flesh is revealed. It is a member of the celery family and has a delicious earthy, nutty flavour.

CREAM OF CELERIAC SOUP

serves 6
prep + cook time
8½ hours
nutritional count per serving
13.3g total fat
(6.7g saturated fat);
995kJ (238 cal);
16.8g carbohydrate;
7.1g protein; 12.6g fibre

Suitable to freeze at the end of step 1.

Be careful when blending or processing hot soup – don't over-fill the container (one-third to half-full as a guide), and make sure the lid is secure.

2kg (4 pounds) celeriac (celery root), chopped coarsely
1 medium brown onion (150g), chopped coarsely
3 cloves garlic, quartered
1 stalk celery (150g), trimmed, chopped coarsely

1.5 litres (6 cups) water
1 litre (4 cups) chicken stock
½ cup (125ml) pouring cream
⅓ cup loosely packed fresh chervil leaves
1 tablespoon olive oil

1 Combine celeriac, onion, garlic, celery, the water and stock in 4.5-litre (18-cup) slow cooker. Cook, covered, on low, 8 hours.
2 Stand soup 10 minutes, then blend or process, in batches, until smooth. Return soup to cooker; stir in cream. Cook, covered, on high, until hot; season to taste.
3 Serve soup sprinkled with chervil; drizzle with oil.

STEWS & CASSEROLES

SPICY TOMATO AND SAFFRON CHICKEN CASSEROLE

serves 6
prep + cook time
6 hours 25 minutes
nutritional count per serving
23.8g total fat
(7.2g saturated fat);
1522kJ (364 cal);
10.2g carbohydrate;
26.5g protein; 2.5g fibre

Suitable to freeze at the
end of step 3.

Serve casserole with steamed
rice or couscous.

Preserved lemon is available
at delicatessens and some
supermarkets. Remove and
discard the lemon flesh,
wash the rind, then use it
as the recipe directs.

¼ cup (35g) plain (all-purpose) flour
2 tablespoons moroccan seasoning
6 chicken thigh cutlets (1.2kg)
1 tablespoon vegetable oil
1 large brown onion (200g), sliced thickly
2 cloves garlic, crushed
2.5cm (1 inch) piece fresh ginger (15g), grated
1 fresh long red chilli, sliced thinly
2 cups (500ml) chicken stock
400g (14½ ounces) canned diced tomatoes
¼ cup (70g) tomato paste
¼ teaspoon saffron threads

PRESERVED LEMON GREMOLATA
⅓ cup finely chopped fresh flat-leaf parsley
1 tablespoon thinly sliced preserved
  lemon rind
1 clove garlic, crushed

1   Combine flour and 1 tablespoon of the seasoning in small shallow bowl; toss chicken in flour mixture to coat, shake off excess. Heat half the oil in large frying pan; cook chicken, in batches, until browned. Transfer to 4.5-litre (18-cup) slow cooker.
2   Heat remaining oil in same pan, add onion, garlic, ginger, chilli and remaining seasoning; cook, stirring, until onion softens. Add ½ cup of the stock; cook, stirring, until mixture boils.
3   Stir onion mixture into cooker with remaining stock, undrained tomatoes, paste and saffron. Cook, covered, on low, 6 hours. Season to taste.
4   Make preserved lemon gremolata before serving.
5   Sprinkle casserole with gremolata.

PRESERVED LEMON GREMOLATA Combine ingredients in small bowl.

Artichoke leaves are pulled off the whole artichoke, one by one, and eaten by scraping against the teeth to extract the soft flesh at the base of each leaf. In this recipe we suggest dipping the leaves in a full-flavoured olive oil and the flavoured crumbs before eating.

ARTICHOKES WITH GARLIC ANCHOVY CRUMBS

6 medium globe artichokes (1.2kg)
2 litres (8 cups) water
2 cups (500ml) chicken stock
2 tablespoons lemon juice
¼ cup (60ml) olive oil

GARLIC ANCHOVY CRUMBS
1 tablespoon olive oil
6 anchovy fillets, drained, chopped finely
3 cloves garlic, crushed
1½ cups (105g) stale breadcrumbs
1 tablespoon finely grated lemon rind
⅓ cup finely chopped fresh flat-leaf parsley
½ cup (40g) finely grated romano cheese

serves 6 (as a starter)
prep + cook time
8 hours 35 minutes
nutritional count per serving
6.2g total fat
(1.8g saturated fat);
648kJ (155 cal);
13.9g carbohydrate;
9.5g protein; 2.3g fibre

Not suitable to freeze.

Serve with some crusty bread and a green or tomato salad to make a main meal.

1 Remove and discard tough outer leaves from artichokes. Trim stems so that artichoke bases sit flat. Using a small teaspoon, remove and discard hairy chokes from centre of artichokes; rinse artichokes under cold water.
2 Pack artichokes tightly, upside down, into 4.5-litre (18-cup) slow cooker; pour in the water, stock and juice. Cook, covered, on low, 8 hours.
3 Make garlic anchovy crumbs before serving.
4 Remove artichokes with slotted spoon; drain well. Serve artichokes with olive oil and garlic anchovy crumbs for dipping.

GARLIC ANCHOVY CRUMBS Heat oil in large frying pan; cook anchovy and garlic, stirring, until anchovy softens. Add breadcrumbs and rind; cook, stirring, until crumbs are browned lightly and crisp. Transfer to medium bowl; cool. Stir in parsley and cheese; season to taste.

Corned beef is a true classic that gets its name from the corn kernel-sized grains of salt that it was packed in to cure it. It is simplicity itself to make, and serving it with a piquant sauce, like horseradish, adds bite to the sweet, gentle saltiness of the meat.

CORNED BEEF WITH HORSERADISH SAUCE

serves 6
prep + cook time
8 hours 10 minutes
nutritional count per serving
26.1g total fat
(13.9g saturated fat);
2266kJ (542 cal);
10.2g carbohydrate;
65.7g protein; 1.4g fibre

Not suitable to freeze.

A mix of steamed seasonal vegetables make a good accompaniment to corned beef: try baby potatoes, carrots, peas or beans, squash or zucchini.

1.5kg (3¼ pound) piece corned silverside
1 medium brown onion (150g),
  chopped coarsely
1 medium carrot (120g), chopped coarsely
1 stalk celery (150g), trimmed,
  chopped coarsely
10 black peppercorns
1 tablespoon brown malt vinegar
1 teaspoon light brown sugar
2.5 litres (10 cups) water, approximately

HORSERADISH SAUCE
45g (1½ ounces) butter
2 tablespoons plain (all-purpose) flour
2 cups (500ml) hot milk
1 tablespoon horseradish cream
1 tablespoon coarsely chopped fresh
  flat-leaf parsley

1 Rinse beef under cold water; pat dry with absorbent paper. Place beef, onion, carrot, celery, peppercorns, vinegar and sugar in 4.5-litre (18-cup) slow cooker. Add enough of the water to barely cover beef. Cook, covered, on low, 8 hours.
2 Make horseradish sauce just before serving.
3 Remove beef from cooker; discard liquid and vegetables.
4 Slice beef thickly; serve with horseradish sauce.

HORSERADISH SAUCE Melt butter in medium saucepan, add flour; cook, stirring, 1 minute. Gradually add milk, stirring, until sauce boils and thickens. Stir in horseradish cream and parsley. Season to taste.

BEST-EVER BOLOGNESE SAUCE

serves 6
prep + cook time
10 hours 40 minutes
nutritional count per serving
16.3g total fat
(5.4g saturated fat);
1576kJ (377 cal);
7.4g carbohydrate;
41.7g protein; 3.5g fibre

Suitable to freeze at the
end of step 2.

Serve with spaghetti or your
favourite pasta; top with
shaved parmesan cheese.

Prosciutto can be replaced
with bacon.

Fresh tomatoes can
be replaced with 800g
(28 ounces) canned
diced tomatoes.

1 tablespoon olive oil
125g (4 ounce) piece prosciutto,
  chopped finely
2 medium brown onions (300g),
  chopped finely
1 large carrot (180g), chopped finely
2 stalks celery (300g), trimmed,
  chopped finely
2 cloves garlic, crushed

500g (1 pound) minced (ground) veal
500g (1 pound) minced (ground) pork
1 cup (250ml) dry red wine
1½ cups (375ml) beef stock
¼ cup (70g) tomato paste
1kg (2 pounds) ripe tomatoes, peeled,
  seeded, chopped coarsely
⅓ cup finely chopped fresh basil
2 tablespoons finely chopped fresh oregano

1 Heat half the oil in large frying pan; cook prosciutto, stirring, until crisp. Add onion, carrot, celery and garlic; cook, stirring, until vegetables soften. Transfer to 4.5-litre (18-cup) slow cooker.
2 Heat remaining oil in same pan; cook minces, stirring, until browned. Add wine; bring to the boil. Stir mince mixture into cooker with stock, paste and tomatoes; cook, covered, on low, 10 hours.
3 Stir in herbs; cook, covered, on high, 10 minutes. Season to taste.

CHICKEN CACCIATORE

2 tablespoons olive oil
12 chicken drumsticks (1.8kg), skin removed
1 medium brown onion (150g), sliced thickly
3 cloves garlic, crushed
3 drained anchovy fillets, crushed
½ cup (125ml) dry white wine
⅓ cup (80ml) chicken stock
⅓ cup (80ml) tomato pasta sauce

2 tablespoons tomato paste
2 teaspoons finely chopped fresh basil
1 teaspoon caster (superfine) sugar
⅓ cup (55g) seeded black olives, halved
1 tablespoon finely chopped fresh
  flat-leaf parsley

serves 6
prep + cook time
6 hours 25 minutes
nutritional count per serving
18.5g total fat
(4.4g saturated fat);
1501kJ (359 cal);
6.9g carbohydrate;
37.2g protein; 1.3g fibre

Suitable to freeze at the
end of step 2.

Serve with creamy mashed
potato or crusty bread.

Use a plain (unflavoured)
tomato-based sauce suitable
for serving over pasta. These
sauces can be bought in cans
and jars and are often
labelled "sugo" or "passata".

1   Heat oil in large frying pan; cook chicken, in batches, until browned all over. Transfer chicken to 4.5-litre (18-cup) slow cooker.
2   Cook onion, garlic and anchovy in same pan, stirring, until onion softens. Add wine; bring to the boil. Boil, uncovered, until reduced by half; stir into cooker with stock, sauce, paste, basil and sugar. Cook, covered, on low, 6 hours.
3   Stir in olives and parsley; season to taste.

The harmony of flavours and perfect balance between savoury and sweet is what makes this dish so uniquely Moroccan. The long, slow cooking and infusion of elaborate spices leaves the lamb meltingly tender and full of sweet, savoury and spicy flavour.

MOROCCAN LAMB WITH KUMARA AND RAISINS

2 tablespoons olive oil
1.2kg (2½ pounds) boned lamb shoulder, chopped coarsely
1 large brown onion (200g), sliced thickly
4 cloves garlic, crushed
2 tablespoons ras el hanout
2 cups (500ml) chicken stock
½ cup (125ml) water
1 tablespoon honey
2 medium kumara (orange sweet potato) (800g), chopped coarsely

400g (15 ounces) canned chickpeas (garbanzo beans), rinsed, drained
1 cinnamon stick
3 cardamom pods, bruised
⅓ cup (50g) raisins, halved
½ cup loosely packed fresh coriander (cilantro) leaves
⅓ cup (55g) coarsely chopped blanched almonds, roasted

serves 6
prep + cook time
6 hours 25 minutes
nutritional count per serving
30.5g total fat
(9.7g saturated fat);
2567kJ (614 cal);
34.9g carbohydrate;
47.2g protein; 6.3g fibre

Suitable to freeze at the end of step 2.

Serve with buttered couscous and steamed green beans.

Ras el hanout is a blend of Moroccan spices; it's available in delis and specialist food stores. If you can't find it, use a Moroccan seasoning available in supermarkets.

1   Heat half the oil in large frying pan; cook lamb, in batches, until browned all over. Remove from pan. Heat remaining oil in same pan; cook onion and garlic, stirring, until onion is soft. Add ras el hanout; cook, stirring, until fragrant. Remove from heat; stir in stock, the water and honey.
2   Place kumara in 4.5-litre (18-cup) slow cooker; stir in chickpeas, cinnamon, cardamom, lamb and onion mixture. Cook, covered, on low, 6 hours. Season to taste.
3   Stir in raisins and coriander; sprinkle with nuts to serve.

LAMB, HARISSA AND CHICKPEA CASSEROLE

serves 6
prep + cook time
7 hours 35 minutes
nutritional count per serving
23.1g total fat
(9g saturated fat);
2019kJ (483 cal);
19.9g carbohydrate;
46.2g protein; 5.5g fibre

Suitable to freeze at the
end of step 3.

Serve with rice pilaf,
steamed rice or couscous.

1.2kg (2½ pounds) boned lamb shoulder,
  chopped coarsely
¼ cup (35g) plain (all-purpose) flour
1 tablespoon olive oil
1 medium red onion (170g), sliced thinly
2 cloves garlic, crushed
2cm (¾ inch) piece fresh ginger (10g), grated

1 teaspoon ground allspice
1½ cups (375ml) beef stock
2 tablespoons harissa paste
2 x 5cm (2 inch) strips orange rind
800g (30 ounces) canned chickpeas
  (garbanzo beans), rinsed, drained
⅓ cup coarsely chopped fresh mint

1 Toss lamb in flour to coat; shake off excess. Heat half the oil in large frying pan; cook lamb, in batches, until browned. Transfer to 4.5-litre (18-cup) slow cooker.
2 Heat remaining oil in same pan; cook onion, garlic and ginger, stirring, until onion softens. Add allspice; cook, stirring, until fragrant. Add ½ cup of the stock; cook, stirring, until mixture boils.
3 Stir onion mixture into cooker with remaining stock, harissa, rind and chickpeas. Cook, covered, on low, 7 hours.
4 Season to taste; sprinkle casserole with mint.

VEAL AND ROSEMARY CASSEROLE

1.2kg (2½ pounds) boned veal shoulder,
    chopped coarsely
¼ cup (35g) plain (all-purpose) flour
1 tablespoon olive oil
1 medium brown onion (150g),
    chopped coarsely
2 cloves garlic, crushed

½ cup (125ml) dry red wine
2 medium carrots (240g), chopped coarsely
2 stalks celery (300g), trimmed,
    chopped coarsely
2 medium parsnips (500g), chopped coarsely
2½ cups (625ml) beef stock
3 sprigs fresh rosemary

serves 6
prep + cook time
8 hours 35 minutes
nutritional count per serving
8.6g total fat
(2g saturated fat);
1513kJ (362 cal);
15.6g carbohydrate;
49.5g protein; 4.2g fibre

Suitable to freeze at the
end of step 3.

Serve casserole with crusty
bread or soft creamy polenta.

The butcher might have
some good stewing veal
available – it's fine to use
in this recipe.

1   Toss veal in flour to coat, shake off excess. Heat half the oil in large frying pan; cook veal, in
batches, until browned. Transfer to 4.5-litre (18-cup) slow cooker.
2   Heat remaining oil in same pan; cook onion and garlic, stirring, until onion softens. Add
wine; bring to the boil. Boil, uncovered, until liquid reduces by half.
3   Stir onion mixture into cooker with carrot, celery, parsnip, stock and rosemary. Cook, covered,
on low, 8 hours. Season to taste.

Italians are the masters of creating delicious meals out of fresh, simple ingredients, and this beef casserole showcases that knack. Take the beef, add some vegetables, fresh herbs and stock, and you have a simple, tasty and hearty meal.

ITALIAN BEEF CASSEROLE

serves 6
prep + cook time
8½ hours
nutritional count per serving
16.8g total fat
(6.2g saturated fat);
1731kJ (414 cal);
12.5g carbohydrate;
47.6g protein; 4g fibre

Suitable to freeze at the end of step 3.

Serve with creamy polenta, mashed potato or pasta.

1.2kg (2½ pounds) beef blade steak, chopped coarsely
¼ cup (35g) plain (all-purpose) flour
1 tablespoon olive oil
1 large brown onion (200g), chopped coarsely
2 cloves garlic, crushed
½ teaspoon dried chilli flakes
½ cup (125ml) dry red wine
400g (14½ ounces) canned diced tomatoes
¼ cup (70g) tomato paste
2½ cups (625ml) beef stock

2 bay leaves
1 large red capsicum (bell pepper) (350g), chopped coarsely
1 tablespoon finely chopped fresh oregano
⅓ cup coarsely chopped fresh basil
1 large zucchini (150g), halved lengthways, sliced thickly
185g (6 ounces) swiss brown mushrooms, halved
⅓ cup loosely packed fresh basil leaves

1 Toss beef in flour to coat, shake off excess. Heat half the oil in large frying pan; cook beef, in batches, until browned. Transfer to 4.5-litre (18-cup) slow cooker.
2 Heat remaining oil in same pan; cook onion, garlic and chilli, stirring, until onion softens. Add wine; bring to the boil. Boil, uncovered, until liquid reduces by half.
3 Stir onion mixture into cooker with undrained tomatoes, paste, stock, bay leaves, capsicum, oregano and the chopped basil. Cook, covered, on low, 8 hours.
4 Add zucchini and mushrooms to cooker for last 30 minutes of cooking time. Discard bay leaves. Season to taste.
5 Sprinkle casserole with basil leaves to serve.

HONEY AND BALSAMIC BRAISED PORK

serves 6
prep + cook time
8 hours
nutritional count per serving
23.6g total fat
(6.5g saturated fat);
1969kJ (471 cal);
20g carbohydrate;
44g protein; 1.1g fibre

Suitable to freeze at the
end of step 3.

Serve pork with mashed
potatoes or soft creamy
polenta, and some wilted
shredded cabbage.

2 tablespoons olive oil
1.2kg (2½ pound) piece pork neck
9 shallots (225g), halved
1½ cups (375ml) chicken stock
⅓ cup (80ml) white balsamic vinegar
¼ cup (90g) honey
6 cloves garlic, peeled
2 sprigs fresh rosemary
1 cup (160g) seeded green olives

1   Heat oil in large frying pan; cook pork until browned all over. Remove from pan.
2   Add shallots to same pan; cook, stirring, until browned all over. Add stock, vinegar
and honey; bring to the boil.
3   Place garlic and rosemary in 4.5-litre (18-cup) slow cooker; top with pork. Pour
over shallot mixture; cook, covered, on low, 7 hours.
4   Add olives; cook, covered, on low, 30 minutes. Season to taste.
5   Remove pork; stand, covered, 10 minutes before slicing. Serve pork drizzled with sauce.

RABBIT WITH SWEET POTATO AND SAGE

1.5kg (3¼ pound) rabbit
12 baby brown onions (300g)
1 medium white sweet potato (450g), chopped coarsely
2 medium potatoes (400g), chopped coarsely
1 cup (250ml) verjuice
1 cup (250ml) chicken stock
2 cloves garlic, sliced thinly
¼ cup loosely packed fresh sage leaves

1   Cut rabbit into six serving-sized pieces. Peel onions, leaving root ends intact.
2   Combine rabbit, onion and remaining ingredients in 4.5-litre (18-cup) slow cooker; cook, covered, on low, 6 hours. Season to taste.
3   Serve rabbit and vegetables drizzled with broth.

serves 6
prep + cook time
6 hours 20 minutes
nutritional count per serving
4.6g total fat
(1.7g saturated fat);
1112kJ (266 cal);
21.6g carbohydrate;
32.6g protein; 3g fibre

Not suitable to freeze.

Serve with crusty bread and steamed beans or broccoli.

Ask the butcher to cut the rabbit into pieces for you.

Verjuice is available in delis and supermarkets, usually in the vinegar aisle. It's made from unripe grapes and has a slightly acidic taste.

SEAFOOD IN ROMESCO SAUCE

serves 6
prep + cook time
4¾ hours
nutritional count per serving
9.5g total fat
(1.2g saturated fat);
1509kJ (361 cal);
9.5g carbohydrate;
57.1g protein;
3.7g fibre

Not suitable to freeze.

Serve with steamed rice
and crusty bread.

Packets of ground almonds
are sometimes sold as almond
meal. They are available
from health-food stores and
most major supermarkets.

1kg (2 pounds) cleaned whole baby octopus

800g (28 ounces) canned crushed tomatoes

4 cloves garlic, crushed

1 teaspoon dried chilli flakes

2 teaspoons smoked paprika

2 medium red capsicums (bell peppers) (400g), sliced thinly

2 tablespoons red wine vinegar

500g (1 pound) uncooked medium king prawns (shrimp)

500g (1 pound) cleaned mussels

½ cup (60g) ground almonds

½ cup coarsely chopped fresh flat-leaf parsley

⅓ cup coarsely chopped fresh oregano

1 Combine octopus, undrained tomatoes, garlic, chilli, paprika, capsicum and vinegar in 4.5-litre (18-cup) slow cooker; cook, covered, on low, 4 hours.

2 Meanwhile, shell and devein prawns, leaving tails intact. Add prawns, mussels and ground almonds to cooker; cook, covered, stirring occasionally, on high, about 20 minutes or until prawns change colour and mussels open (discard any that do not.)

3 Serve sprinkled with herbs.

For best results, get the butcher to cut the ribs into individual pieces. They become more tender and fit more easily into the slow cooker.

Stout is a strong-flavoured, dark-coloured type of beer, originally from Britain. It is made with roasted barley, giving it its characteristic dark colour and bitter-sweet, almost coffee-like, flavour.

BEEF RIBS WITH STOUT AND CARAMELISED ONION

serves 6
prep + cook time
8¾ hours
nutritional count per serving
21.4g total fat
(8.1g saturated fat);
2228kJ (533 cal);
12g carbohydrate;
67.2g protein; 3.5g fibre

Suitable to freeze at the end of step 3.

Serve ribs with steamed rice and a green leafy salad.

1 tablespoon olive oil
2.5kg (5¼ pounds) racks beef short ribs
2 large brown onions (400g), sliced thinly
1 tablespoon light brown sugar
1 tablespoon balsamic vinegar
¼ cup (60ml) water

3 medium carrots (360g), sliced thickly
400g (14½ ounces) canned diced tomatoes
5 sprigs fresh thyme
1 tablespoon dijon mustard
1 cup (250ml) beef stock
1 cup (250ml) stout

1 Heat half the oil in large frying pan; cook ribs, in batches, until browned. Remove from pan.
2 Heat remaining oil in large frying pan; cook onion, stirring, until soft. Add sugar, vinegar and the water; cook, stirring occasionally, about 10 minutes or until onion caramelises.
3 Transfer onion mixture to 4.5-litre (18-cup) slow cooker; stir in carrot, undrained tomatoes, thyme, mustard, stock and stout. Add ribs, turn to coat in sauce mixture. Cook, covered, on low, 8 hours. Season to taste.
4 Cut ribs into serving-sized pieces; serve with the sauce.

Beef brisket is an economical cut of meat; ask the butcher to trim the fat away and to chop the meat for you.

For a slightly richer colour and flavour, brown the beef in a little oil in a frying pan before adding it to the slow cooker.

Any type of white beans can be used; navy, great northern or haricot are all good choices.

CHILLI AND BRANDY BEEF WITH WHITE BEANS

6 shallots (150g)
1.2kg (2½ pounds) beef brisket, chopped coarsely
1 fresh long red chilli, chopped finely
2 cloves garlic, crushed
3 medium egg (plum) tomatoes (225g), chopped coarsely

2 tablespoons tomato paste
1 cup (250ml) beef stock
¼ cup (60ml) brandy
400g (15 ounces) canned cannellini beans, rinsed, drained
⅓ cup coarsely chopped fresh flat-leaf parsley

serves 6
prep + cook time
8 hours 25 minutes
nutritional count per serving
12.1g total fat
(5.1g saturated fat);
1375kJ (329 cal);
3.6g carbohydrate;
45g protein; 2.2g fibre

Suitable to freeze at the end of step 2.

This recipe is quite hearty, so a simple green salad or crusty bread would go well as an accompaniment.

1 Peel shallots, leaving root ends intact; cut shallots in half lengthways.
2 Combine shallot, beef, chilli, garlic, tomato, paste, stock and brandy in 4.5-litre (18-cup) slow cooker; cook, covered, on low, 8 hours.
3 Add beans; cook, covered, on high, about 20 minutes or until hot. Stir in parsley; season to taste.

The Chinese hot pot boasts a history of more than 1000 years. Traditionally, the hot pot consisted of a metal pot filled with simmering stock that was placed in the centre of the dining table. The ingredients, which varied greatly from region to region in China, were added and cooked at the table.

CHINESE CHICKEN HOT POT

serves 6
prep + cook time
8 hours 20 minutes
nutritional count per serving
25.2g total fat
(7.9g saturated fat);
2077kJ (487 cal);
20.8g carbohydrate;
34.8g protein; 1.7g fibre

Suitable to freeze at the end of step 1.

Serve with steamed fresh rice noodles or rice.

Chinese cooking wine is also known as chinese rice wine and shao hsing wine. Dry sherry can be used instead.

1.8kg (3¾ pound) whole chicken
1 litre (4 cups) water
1 litre (4 cups) chicken stock
2 cups (500ml) chinese cooking wine
½ cup (125ml) light soy sauce
⅓ cup (80ml) oyster sauce
⅓ cup (75g) firmly packed light brown sugar
4 cloves garlic, bruised
6cm (2¼ inch) piece fresh ginger (30g), sliced thinly
3 star anise
1 teaspoon five-spice powder
2 fresh long red chillies, halved lengthways
500g (1 pound) baby buk choy, chopped coarsely
⅓ cup coarsely chopped fresh coriander (cilantro)
1 fresh long red chilli, extra, sliced thinly

1   Rinse chicken under cold water; pat dry, inside and out, with absorbent paper. Combine the water, stock, cooking wine, sauces, sugar, garlic, ginger, spices and chilli in 4.5-litre (18-cup) slow cooker. Add chicken; cook, covered, on low, 8 hours.
2   Remove chicken; strain broth through fine sieve into large bowl. Discard solids. Cover chicken to keep warm. Return broth to cooker. Add buk choy to cooker; cook, covered, on high, about 5 minutes or until tender.
3   Cut chicken into 6 pieces; serve with buk choy, drizzle with the broth. Sprinkle with coriander and extra chilli.

COQ AU VIN

20 spring onions (500g)
2 tablespoons olive oil
6 rindless bacon slices (390g), sliced thinly
440g (14 ounces) button mushrooms
2 cloves garlic, crushed
1.8kg (3¾ pound) whole chicken
2 cups (500ml) dry red wine
2 medium carrots (240g), chopped coarsely

3 bay leaves
4 sprigs fresh thyme
2 sprigs fresh rosemary
1½ cups (375ml) chicken stock
¼ cup (70g) tomato paste
¼ cup (35g) cornflour (cornstarch)
2 tablespoons water

1   Trim green ends from onions, leaving about 4cm (1½ inches) of stem attached; trim roots leaving onions intact. Heat half the oil in large frying pan; cook onions, stirring, until browned all over, remove from pan. Add bacon, mushrooms and garlic to same pan; cook, stirring, until bacon is crisp, remove from pan.
2   Cut chicken into 12 pieces. Heat remaining oil in same pan; cook chicken, in batches, until browned all over; drain on absorbent paper. Add wine to same pan; bring to the boil, stirring.
3   Place chicken in 4.5-litre (18-cup) slow cooker with onions, bacon and mushroom mixture, carrot, herbs, stock, wine mixture and paste. Cook, covered, on low, 7 hours.
4   Stir in blended cornflour and the water; cook, covered, on high, about 20 minutes or until sauce thickens slightly. Season to taste.

serves 6
prep + cook time
8 hours
nutritional count per serving
39.6g total fat
(11.7g saturated fat);
2750kJ (658 cal);
12.3g carbohydrate;
47.8g protein; 5.1g fibre

Not suitable to freeze.

Serve with creamy mashed potato drizzled with some of the sauce; accompany with a green salad.

Use chicken pieces if you prefer, such as 6 thigh cutlets and 6 drumsticks or 6 marylands, or ask your butcher to cut the whole chicken into 12 serving pieces for you.

Use shallots instead of spring onions, if you like.

The swede and parsnip used in this stew give it a particularly thick, hearty quality. Swede, also known as rutabaga and swedish turnip, is a winter root vegetable; it has a distinctive smell when cooking, a white flesh that becomes golden when cooked, and a lovely, sweet flavour.

SIMPLE BEEF AND VEGETABLE CASSEROLE

serves 6
prep + cook time
8½ hours
nutritional count per serving
18.7g total fat
(5.2g saturated fat);
1827kJ (437 cal);
19.3g carbohydrate;
44.9g protein; 5.9g fibre

Suitable to freeze at the end of step 3.

Serve with crusty bread.

Use whatever vegetables you like: turnip, celeriac, jerusalem artichokes are all good choices.

Gravy beef can be used instead of chuck steak.

1.2kg (2½ pounds) beef chuck steak, chopped coarsely
⅓ cup (50g) plain (all-purpose) flour
¼ cup (60ml) olive oil
2 medium brown onions (300g), cut into thick wedges
2 medium carrots (240g), chopped coarsely
2 stalks celery (300g), trimmed, chopped coarsely
1 medium parsnip (250g), chopped coarsely

1 medium swede (rutabaga) (225g), chopped coarsely
3 cloves garlic, crushed
¼ cup (70g) tomato paste
400g (14½ ounces) canned crushed tomatoes
1 cup (250ml) beef stock
2 bay leaves
10 sprigs fresh thyme

1 Coat beef in flour; shake off excess. Heat 2 tablespoons of the oil in large frying pan; cook beef, in batches, until browned all over. Transfer beef to 4.5-litre (18-cup) slow cooker.

2 Heat remaining oil in same pan; cook onion, carrot, celery, parsnip, swede and garlic; stirring, until onion softens. Add paste; cook, stirring, 1 minute. Remove from heat; stir in undrained tomatoes and stock.

3 Stir vegetable mixture and bay leaves into cooker; add thyme. Cook, covered, on low, 8 hours. Discard thyme and bay leaves; season to taste.

CREAMY TURKEY STEW WITH MUSTARD

serves 8
prep + cook time
2½ hours
nutritional count per serving
23.2g total fat
(8.8g saturated fat);
1914kJ (458 cal);
5.3g carbohydrate;
53.2g protein; 3.1g fibre

Not suitable to freeze.

Serve with mashed potato and steamed green beans.

Use 3kg turkey marylands if you can't get drumsticks.

4 turkey drumsticks (3kg), skin removed
2 tablespoons olive oil
375g (12 ounces) button mushrooms
2 medium leeks (700g), sliced thickly
4 rindless bacon slices (260g), chopped coarsely
2 cloves garlic, crushed
2 tablespoons plain (all-purpose) flour

1 cup (250ml) chicken stock
½ cup (125ml) dry white wine
2 tablespoons wholegrain (seedless) mustard
6 sprigs fresh lemon thyme
½ cup (125ml) pouring cream
2 teaspoons fresh lemon thyme leaves

1 Using sharp heavy knife, cut turkey meat from bones, chop meat coarsely; discard bones.
2 Heat oil in large frying pan; cook turkey, in batches, until browned all over. Transfer turkey to 4.5-litre (18-cup) slow cooker.
3 Add mushrooms, leek, bacon and garlic to same pan; cook, stirring, until leek softens. Add flour; cook, stirring, 1 minute. Stir in stock, wine, mustard and thyme sprigs; bring to the boil. Boil, uncovered, 2 minutes. Remove from heat; stir in cream. Transfer mushroom mixture to cooker. Cook, covered, on low, 2 hours.
4 Season to taste; sprinkle with thyme leaves.

HUNGARIAN VEAL GOULASH

1kg (2 pounds) boned veal shoulder,
  chopped coarsely
¼ cup (35g) plain (all-purpose) flour
1 tablespoon sweet paprika
2 teaspoons caraway seeds
½ teaspoon cayenne pepper
2 tablespoons olive oil
15g (½ ounce) butter
1 large brown onion (200g), chopped coarsely

2 cloves garlic, crushed
2 tablespoons tomato paste
1½ cups (375ml) beef stock
400g (14½ ounces) canned crushed tomatoes
3 small potatoes (360g), quartered
2 medium carrots (240g), chopped coarsely
½ cup coarsely chopped fresh flat-leaf parsley
½ cup (120g) sour cream

serves 6
prep + cook time
8½ hours
nutritional count per serving
20.7g total fat
(8.7g saturated fat);
1835kJ (439 cal);
18.4g carbohydrate;
42.6g protein; 4.1g fibre

Suitable to freeze at the
end of step 2.

Serve goulash with crusty
bread, rice or pasta.

The butcher might have
some good stewing veal
available – it's fine to use
in this recipe.

1   Toss veal in combined flour and spices to coat; shake away excess flour. Heat half the oil
and half the butter in large frying pan; cook veal, in batches, until browned all over. Transfer
to 4.5-litre (18-cup) slow cooker.
2   Heat remaining oil and butter in same pan; cook onion and garlic, stirring, until onion is
soft. Stir in paste and stock; bring to the boil. Stir into cooker with undrained tomatoes, potato
and carrot; cook, covered, on low, 8 hours.
3   Season to taste; dollop with sour cream and sprinkle with parsley to serve.

The "hand" of pickled pork is a portion of leg and breast. You might need to order this from the butcher in advance. Before the days of refrigeration, pickling meat was a common way to preserve it. The meat, infused with the brine, becomes lovely and tender and breaks apart with a fork.

PICKLED PORK

3kg (6½ pound) hand of pickled pork
2 tablespoons brown malt vinegar
2 bay leaves
1 teaspoon black peppercorns
2 tablespoons dark brown sugar
1.5 litres (6 cups) water, approximately

1   Place pork, vinegar, bay leaves, peppercorns, and sugar in 4.5-litre (18-cup) slow cooker; add enough of the water to barely cover pork. Cook, covered, on low, 8 hours.
2   Carefully remove pork from cooking liquid; cover, stand 10 minutes before slicing. Discard cooking liquid.

serves 6
prep + cook time
8 hours 10 minutes
nutritional count per serving
27.8g total fat
(10.7g saturated fat);
2801kJ (670 cal);
4.2g carbohydrate;
100.7g protein; 0g fibre

Not suitable to freeze.

Pickled pork is delicious served hot with mashed potato, wilted cabbage and mustard, or serve it cold (like ham) with potato salad or coleslaw.

Ask the butcher for either veal or beef shin (osso buco); veal will be smaller than beef, in which case you will need about 12 pieces to serve six people. You can use a mixture of mushrooms as we have, or just one variety with a good robust flavour – you need a total of 500g (1 pound).

OSSO BUCO WITH MIXED MUSHROOMS

serves 6
prep + cook time
8 hours 50 minutes
nutritional count per serving
16.5g total fat
(7.1g saturated fat);
1902kJ (455 cal);
17.4g carbohydrate;
45.5g protein; 3.7g fibre

Not suitable to freeze.

Serve with a mash – potato, celeriac or kumara are all good choices – and a green leafy salad.

6 large pieces beef osso buco (1.7kg)
¼ cup (35g) plain (all-purpose) flour
2 tablespoons olive oil
1 large brown onion (200g), chopped coarsely
1 cup (250ml) marsala
1½ cups (375ml) beef stock
¼ cup (60ml) worcestershire sauce
2 tablespoons wholegrain mustard
2 sprigs fresh rosemary
185g (6 ounces) swiss brown mushrooms, sliced thickly

155g (5 ounces) portabello mushrooms, cut into 8 wedges
155g (5 ounces) oyster mushrooms, chopped coarsely
½ cup (125ml) pouring cream
¼ cup (35g) gravy powder
2 tablespoons water
½ cup coarsely chopped fresh flat-leaf parsley

1 Coat beef all over in flour, shake off excess. Heat half the oil in large frying pan; cook beef, in batches, until browned all over. Remove from pan.
2 Heat remaining oil in same pan; cook onion, stirring, until onion softens. Add marsala; bring to the boil. Add onion mixture to 4.5-litre (18-cup) slow cooker; stir in stock, sauce, mustard and rosemary. Place beef in cooker, fitting pieces upright and tightly packed in a single layer. Add mushrooms to cooker. Cook, covered, on low, 8 hours.
3 Carefully remove beef from cooker; cover to keep warm. Add cream and combined gravy powder and the water to cooker; cook, covered, on high, 10 minutes or until mixture thickens slightly. Stir in parsley; season to taste.
4 Serve beef with mushroom sauce.

RATATOUILLE

serves 6
prep + cook time
4 hours 20 minutes
nutritional count per serving
7.5g total fat
(1g saturated fat);
803kJ (192 cal);
22.1g carbohydrate;
5.5g protein; 7g fibre

Suitable to freeze at the
end of step 2, although it's
much better eaten straight
after cooking.

Serve with creamy polenta.

Use a plain (unflavoured)
tomato-based sauce suitable
for serving over pasta. These
sauces can be bought in cans
and jars and are often
labelled "sugo" or "passata".

2 tablespoons olive oil

1 large red onion (300g), chopped coarsely

3 cloves garlic, crushed

½ cup loosely packed fresh basil leaves

2 tablespoons tomato paste

3 cups (700g) bottled tomato pasta sauce

2 teaspoons caster (superfine) sugar

1 large eggplant (500g), chopped coarsely

2 medium red capsicum (bell pepper) (400g), chopped coarsely

2 large zucchini (300g), chopped coarsely

1 medium green capsicum (200g), chopped coarsely

1 Heat oil in large frying pan; cook onion, garlic and half the basil, stirring, until onion
softens. Add paste; cook, stirring, 1 minute. Remove from heat, stir in pasta sauce and sugar.
2 Place vegetables and sauce mixture into 4.5-litre (18-cup) slow cooker. Cook, covered, on
low, 4 hours. Season to taste.
3 Serve ratatouille sprinkled with remaining basil.

VEAL WITH PARSLEY AND CAPERS

1.2kg (2½ pounds) boned veal shoulder, chopped coarsely
⅓ cup (50g) plain (all-purpose) flour
¼ cup (60ml) olive oil
8 shallots (200g)
375g (12 ounces) button mushrooms
1 cup (250ml) dry white wine
4 bacon bones (320g)

1 cup (250ml) chicken stock
4 bay leaves
1 cup (120g) frozen peas, thawed
1 cup coarsely chopped fresh flat-leaf parsley
1 tablespoon rinsed, drained baby capers
2 teaspoons finely grated lemon rind
2 cloves garlic, chopped finely

serves 6
prep + cook time
6½ hours
nutritional count per serving
16.5g total fat
(3.4g saturated fat);
1814kJ (434 cal);
9.1g carbohydrate;
53.4g protein; 4g fibre

Not suitable to freeze.

Serve with mashed potato and a green leafy salad.

The butcher might have some good stewing veal available – it's fine to use in this recipe.

1   Coat veal in flour; shake off excess. Heat 2 tablespoons of the oil in large frying pan; cook veal, in batches, until browned all over. Transfer veal to 4.5-litre (18-cup) slow cooker.
2   Meanwhile, peel shallots, leave roots intact. Heat remaining oil in same pan; cook shallots and mushrooms, stirring, until browned. Add wine, bring to the boil; boil, uncovered, until reduced by half.
3   Add bacon bones, stock, bay leaves and shallot mixture to cooker. Cook, covered, on low, 6 hours.
4   Discard bacon bones and bay leaves. Stir in peas, parsley, capers, rind and garlic; season to taste.

BRAISED BEEF CHEEKS IN STOUT

2 tablespoons olive oil
6 beef cheeks (1.5kg)
12 shallots (300g)
2 cloves garlic, crushed
1 cup (250ml) beef stock
2 medium carrots (240g), chopped coarsely
250g portabello mushrooms, chopped coarsely
3 cups (750ml) stout
2 tablespoons dark brown sugar
2 sprigs fresh rosemary
¼ cup (35g) cornflour (cornstarch)
2 tablespoons water

serves 6
prep + cook time
9¾ hours
nutritional count per serving
26.2g total fat
(9.4g saturated fat);
2424kJ (580 cal);
16.8g carbohydrate;
55.7g protein; 2.8g fibre

1   Heat half the oil in large frying pan; cook beef, in batches, until browned all over. Transfer to 4.5-litre (18-cup) slow cooker.
2   Meanwhile, peel shallots, trim roots, leaving shallots whole; halve shallots lengthways.
3   Heat remaining oil in same pan; cook shallots and garlic, stirring, until shallots are browned lightly. Add stock; bring to the boil. Stir shallot mixture into cooker with carrot, mushrooms, stout, sugar and rosemary. Cook, covered, on low, 9 hours.
4   Carefully remove beef from cooker; cover to keep warm. Stir blended cornflour and the water into cooker; cook, covered, on high, about 15 minutes or until thickened slightly. Season to taste.
5   Serve beef with sauce.

Not suitable to freeze.

Serve with creamy mashed potato or colcannon (mashed potatoes with cabbage).

Beef cheeks are available from most butchers, but you might need to order them in advance. Substitute beef shin, chuck or blade steak if cheeks are unavailable.

Stout is a strong-flavoured, dark-coloured beer made from barley.

RED WINE, BEEF AND MUSHROOM STEW

serves 6
prep + cook time
8 hours 25 minutes
nutritional count per serving
21.3g total fat
(6.8g saturated fat);
1952kJ (467 cal);
6.3g carbohydrate;
53.1g protein; 5.2g fibre

Not suitable to freeze.

Serve stew over creamy
polenta or mashed potato;
accompany with steamed
green beans.

Chuck steak or any stewing
steak can be used instead of
the gravy beef.

16 spring onions (400g)
2 tablespoons olive oil
375g (12 ounces) button mushrooms
4 rindless bacon slices (260g), chopped coarsely
3 cloves garlic, crushed
1 cup (250ml) dry red wine
¼ cup (70g) tomato paste
½ teaspoon caster (superfine) sugar
1.2kg (2½ pounds) gravy beef, chopped coarsely
2 medium fennel bulbs (600g), sliced thickly
⅓ cup coarsely chopped fresh flat-leaf parsley

1   Trim green ends from onions, leaving about 8cm (3 inches) of stems attached; trim roots.
Heat oil in large frying pan; cook onions, mushrooms, bacon and garlic, stirring, until onion
softens. Stir in wine, paste and sugar; bring to the boil, boil, uncovered, 2 minutes.
2   Place beef, fennel and onion mixture in 4.5-litre (18-cup) slow cooker. Cook, covered,
on low, 8 hours.
3   Stir in parsley; season to taste.

CREAMY POTATO BAKE

1 tablespoon olive oil
2 medium leeks (700g), sliced thinly
4 rindless bacon slices (260g), chopped finely
2 tablespoons coarsely chopped fresh flat-leaf parsley
1.5kg (3¼ pounds) potatoes, sliced thinly
2 cups (500ml) pouring cream
¼ cup (60ml) milk
1 tablespoon dijon mustard
50g packet dried chicken noodle soup mix
½ cup (60g) coarsely grated cheddar cheese
½ cup (40g) finely grated parmesan cheese

1 Heat oil in large frying pan; cook leek and bacon, stirring, until leek softens. Remove from heat; stir in parsley.
2 Layer one third of the potato in 4.5-litre (18-cup) slow cooker; top with half the leek mixture. Repeat layering with remaining potato and leek, finishing with potato layer.
3 Combine cream, milk, mustard and soup mix in large jug, pour over potatoes; sprinkle with combined cheeses. Cook, covered, on low, 6 hours.

serves 8
(as an accompaniment)
prep + cook time
6 hours 25 minutes
nutritional count per serving
38.7g total fat
(22.7g saturated fat);
2257kJ (540 cal);
29.5g carbohydrate;
17.3g protein; 4.3g fibre

Not suitable to freeze.

Serve spoonfuls of the bake with a green leafy salad as a light meal, or as an accompaniment to a main course.

It's important to slice the potatoes thinly; a mandolin or V-slicer makes the job quick and easy.

Instead of the cannellini beans, you can use any canned white beans you like, such as great northern, navy or haricot. Use a plain (unflavoured) tomato-based sauce suitable for serving over pasta. These sauces can be bought in cans and jars and are often labelled "sugo" or "passata".

CHILLI BEANS WITH TOMATO SAUCE

serves 6
prep + cook time
8½ hours
nutritional count per serving
12.9g total fat
(3.9g saturated fat);
1112kJ (266 cal);
17.8g carbohydrate;
17.3g protein; 5.2g fibre

Suitable to freeze at the end of step 1.

Serve with toasted sourdough or cornbread.

1 tablespoon olive oil
6 rindless bacon slices (390g), chopped finely
1 stalk celery (150g), trimmed, chopped finely
1 small brown onion (80g), chopped finely
1 small carrot (70g), chopped finely
1 fresh long red chilli, chopped finely
¼ cup (70g) tomato paste

3 cups (700g) bottled tomato pasta sauce
¾ cup (180ml) chicken stock
2 teaspoons caster (superfine) sugar
800g (30 ounces) canned cannellini beans, rinsed, drained
¼ cup coarsely chopped fresh flat-leaf parsley

1   Heat oil in medium frying pan; cook bacon, celery, onion, carrot and chilli, stirring, until onion softens. Add paste; cook, stirring, 1 minute. Transfer mixture to 4.5-litre (18-cup) slow cooker. Stir in sauce, stock, sugar and beans. Cook, covered, on low, 8 hours.

2   Stir in parsley; season to taste.

HONEY SOY LAMB CHOPS

serves 6
prep + cook time
6 hours 40 minutes
nutritional count per serving
16.9g total fat
(8.2g saturated fat);
1588kJ (380cal);
19.5g carbohydrate;
36.2g protein; 1.6g fibre

Suitable to freeze at the
end of step 2.

Steamed kipfler potatoes,
baby peas and carrots make
a great accompaniment.

¼ cup (60ml) salt-reduced soy sauce
¼ cup (90g) honey
3 cloves garlic, crushed
1 teaspoon sesame oil
2 large red onions (600g), cut into thick wedges
6 lamb forequarter chops (1.2kg)
6 sprigs fresh rosemary
15g (½ ounce) butter, melted
1 tablespoon plain (all-purpose) flour

1   Combine sauce, honey, garlic and oil in small jug.
2   Place onion in 4.5-litre (18-cup) slow cooker; top with lamb, soy sauce mixture
and rosemary. Cook, covered, on low, 6 hours.
3   Discard rosemary, remove lamb from cooker; cover to keep warm.
4   Combine butter and flour in small bowl; stir into cooker. Cook, covered, on high,
about 25 minutes or until sauce thickens; season to taste. Strain sauce through fine sieve
into medium heatproof jug; discard onion.
5   Serve lamb drizzled with sauce.

LAMB AND POTATO STEW WITH SPINACH

3 medium potatoes (600g), unpeeled, cut into thick wedges
2 large brown onions (400g), sliced thickly
2 large carrots (360g), sliced thickly
4 cloves garlic, sliced thinly
1.2kg (2½ pounds) boned lamb leg, chopped coarsely
1½ cups (375ml) chicken stock
1⅔ cups (410g) canned tomato puree
4 sprigs fresh thyme
60g (2 ounces) baby spinach leaves

1   Place potatoes, onion, carrot, garlic and lamb in 4.5-litre (18-cup) slow cooker;
stir in stock, puree and thyme. Cook, covered, on low, 6 hours.
2   Discard thyme. Stir in spinach leaves; season to taste.

serves 6
prep + cook time
6 hours 20 minutes
nutritional count per serving
11.4g total fat
(4.9g saturated fat);
1676kJ (401 cal);
21.6g carbohydrate;
49.6g protein; 5.9g fibre

Not suitable to freeze.

Serve with crusty bread and
steamed green vegetables.

Harissa is a North African paste made from dried red chillies, garlic, olive oil and caraway seeds. It can be used as a rub for meat, a condiment or, most commonly, an ingredient. Coriander usually comes with its roots attached, as the stems and roots of coriander are often used in cooking. Wash under cold water, removing any dirt clinging to the roots then chop roots and stems together to obtain the amount specified.

LAMB TAGINE WITH HARISSA AND GREEN OLIVES

serves 6
prep + cook time
4 hours 35 minutes
nutritional count per serving
32g total fat
(10.2g saturated fat);
2424kJ (580 cal);
26.3g carbohydrate;
44.1g protein; 5.7g fibre

Suitable to freeze at the end of step 3. The lamb mixture can be marinated overnight at the end of step 1.

Serve tagine with couscous flavoured with chopped preserved lemon rind and coarsely chopped fresh mint leaves.

Preserved lemon rind is available at delis and some supermarkets. Remove and discard the flesh, wash the rind, then use it as the recipe directs.

1.2kg (2½ pounds) boned lamb shoulder, chopped coarsely
1 large red onion (300g), grated coarsely
2 cloves garlic, crushed
2 tablespoons finely chopped coriander (cilantro) root and stem mixture
1 cinnamon stick, halved
1 teaspoon ground cumin
1 teaspoon ground ginger
1 teaspoon sweet paprika
⅓ cup (80ml) olive oil
1 tablespoon harissa

800g (28 ounces) canned diced tomatoes
¼ cup (70g) tomato paste
½ cup (125ml) beef stock
400g (15 ounces) canned chickpeas (garbanzo beans), rinsed, drained
2 tablespoons honey
½ cup (90g) seeded small green olives
2 teaspoons finely chopped preserved lemon rind
½ cup loosely packed fresh mint leaves

1 Combine lamb, onion, garlic, coriander root and stem mixture, spices and half the oil in large bowl.
2 Heat remaining oil in large frying pan; cook lamb, in batches, until browned all over. Transfer lamb to 4.5-litre (18-cup) slow cooker.
3 Stir harissa, undrained tomatoes, paste, stock, chickpeas and honey into cooker. Cook, covered, on low, 4 hours.
4 Remove cinnamon stick; stir in olives and lemon rind. Season to taste; sprinkle with mint.

CHORIZO, CHILLI AND BEAN STEW

serves 6
prep + cook time
3 hours 20 minutes
nutritional count per serving
28.7g total fat
(9.6g saturated fat);
1689kJ (404 cal);
13.1g carbohydrate;
21.3g protein; 5.8g fibre

Suitable to freeze at the
end of step 2.

Serve with a green salad and
some crusty bread.

1 tablespoon olive oil

1 large red onion (300g), chopped coarsely

3 chorizo sausages (500g), chopped coarsely

4 cloves garlic, crushed

1 teaspoon dried chilli flakes

1 medium red capsicum (bell pepper) (200g), chopped coarsely

150g baby green beans, halved

800g (30 ounces) canned cannellini beans, rinsed, drained

800g (28 ounces) canned diced tomatoes

⅓ cup (80ml) chicken stock

2 bay leaves

⅓ cup coarsely chopped fresh flat-leaf parsley

1   Heat oil in large frying pan; cook onion and chorizo, stirring, until browned lightly.
Add garlic and chilli flakes; cook, stirring, until fragrant.
2   Combine capsicum, both beans, undrained tomatoes, stock, bay leaves and chorizo
mixture in 4.5-litre (18-cup) slow cooker. Cook, covered, on low, 3 hours.
3   Discard bay leaves. Season to taste; sprinkle with parsley.

Check with the butcher to make sure the tripe has been cleaned and blanched. We suggest you blanch the tripe again (see step 1) before cutting it into pieces. You might have to order the tripe from the butcher in advance.

Use a plain (unflavoured) tomato-based sauce suitable for serving over pasta. These sauces can be bought in cans and jars and are often labelled "sugo" or "passata".

TOMATO TRIPE STEW WITH PANCETTA

1.5kg (3¼ pounds) honeycomb tripe
1 tablespoon olive oil
1 medium brown onion (150g), chopped coarsely
2 cloves garlic, crushed
6 slices pancetta (90g), chopped coarsely
⅓ cup (80ml) dry white wine
1 large carrot (180g), chopped coarsely
1 stalk celery (150g), trimmed, chopped coarsely
3 cups (700g) bottled tomato pasta sauce
2 bay leaves
½ cup coarsely chopped fresh flat-leaf parsley

serves 6
prep + cook time
6½ hours
nutritional count per serving
11.3g total fat
(3.6g saturated fat);
1371kJ (328 cal);
14g carbohydrate;
38.3g protein; 3.9g fibre

Not suitable to freeze.

Serve stew with crusty bread.

1   Cover tripe with cold water in large saucepan; bring to the boil. Boil, covered, 10 minutes. Drain. Cut tripe into 4cm (1½ inch) pieces, transfer to 4.5-litre (18-cup) slow cooker.
2   Meanwhile, heat oil in small frying pan; cook onion, garlic and pancetta, stirring, until onion softens and pancetta is browned and crisp.
3   Transfer onion mixture to cooker; stir in wine, carrot, celery, sauce and bay leaves. Cook, covered, on low, 6 hours.
4   Discard bay leaves. Season to taste. Sprinkle stew with parsley.

ROASTS

CHICKEN WITH LEEKS AND ARTICHOKES

serves 4
prep + cook time
6½ hours
nutritional count per serving
42.2g total fat
(16.3g saturated fat);
2571kJ (615 cal);
5.6g carbohydrate;
44.9g protein; 4.2g fibre

Not suitable to freeze.

Serve chicken with creamy mashed potatoes and a green leafy salad.

Replace the baby leeks with 1 large leek (500g), sliced thickly.

1.6kg (3¼ pound) whole chicken
1 unpeeled lemon, chopped coarsely
4 cloves unpeeled garlic
4 sprigs fresh tarragon
6 sprigs fresh flat-leaf parsley
45g (1½ ounces) butter
¾ cup (180ml) dry white wine
2 medium globe artichokes (400g), quartered
8 baby leeks (640g)
1 cup (250ml) chicken stock

1 Wash chicken under cold water; pat dry inside and out with absorbent paper. Place lemon, garlic and herbs in chicken cavity; season with salt and pepper. Tuck wing tips under chicken; tie legs together with kitchen string.
2 Melt butter in large frying pan; cook chicken until browned all over. Remove chicken. Add wine; bring to the boil.
3 Meanwhile, trim stems from artichokes; remove tough outer leaves. Place artichokes and leeks in 4.5-litre (18-cup) slow cooker; add wine mixture and stock. Place chicken on vegetables; cook, covered, on low, 6 hours.
4 Serve chicken with vegetables; drizzle with a little of the juice.

BEEF POT ROAST

¼ cup (60ml) olive oil
4 small potatoes (180g), unpeeled, halved
375g (12 ounce) piece unpeeled pumpkin, cut into 4 wedges
8 baby onions (200g), halved
375g (12 ounces) baby carrots
250g (8 ounces) jerusalem artichokes (sunchokes)
750g (1½ pound) piece beef blade steak

1 tablespoon wholegrain mustard
2 teaspoons smoked paprika
2 teaspoons finely chopped fresh rosemary
1 clove garlic, crushed
1½ cups (375ml) beef stock
½ cup (125ml) dry red wine
2 tablespoons balsamic vinegar
¼ cup (35g) gravy powder
2 tablespoons water

serves 4
prep + cook time
8½ hours
nutritional count per serving
26.8g total fat
(7.5g saturated fat);
2353kJ (563 cal);
25g carbohydrate;
46.8g protein; 7.1g fibre

Not suitable to freeze.

Serve with steamed green beans or broccoli.

We used nicola potatoes and jap pumpkin in this recipe.

Jerusalem artichokes can be hard to find. You can leave them out and add swede, parsnip or turnip to the pot roast instead.

Gravy powder is an instant gravy mix made with browned flour. Plain (all-purpose) flour can be used for thickening instead.

1 Heat 2 tablespoons of the oil in large frying pan; cook potato, pumpkin and onion, in batches, until browned all over. Place vegetables in 4.5-litre (18-cup) slow cooker with carrots and artichokes.
2 Heat 2 teaspoons of the remaining oil in same pan; cook beef until browned all over. Remove beef from pan; spread with combined mustard, paprika, rosemary, garlic and remaining oil.
3 Place beef on vegetables in slow cooker; pour over combined stock, wine and vinegar. Cook, covered, on low, 8 hours.
4 Remove beef and vegetables from cooker; cover beef, stand 10 minutes before slicing thinly. Cover vegetables to keep warm.
5 Meanwhile, blend gravy powder with the water in small bowl until smooth. Stir gravy mixture into liquid in slow cooker; cook, covered, on high, about 10 minutes or until gravy is thickened slightly. Season to taste. Strain gravy.
6 Serve beef with gravy and vegetables.

GREEN OLIVE AND LEMON CHICKEN

serves 4
prep + cook time
6 hours 20 minutes
nutritional count per serving
38.1g total fat
(12.1g saturated fat);
2086kJ (499 cal);
2g carbohydrate;
37.7g protein; 0.6g fibre

Not suitable to freeze.

Serve chicken with roasted
potatoes and steamed green
vegetables, or creamy polenta
or mash, and a green salad.

Kitchen string is made of
a natural product such as
cotton or hemp so that it
neither affects the flavour
of the food it's tied around
nor melts when heated.

15g (½ ounce) butter, softened
1 tablespoon olive oil
2 teaspoons finely grated lemon rind
3 cloves garlic, crushed
¼ cup (30g) seeded green olives, chopped finely
2 tablespoons finely chopped fresh flat-leaf parsley
1.5kg (3¼ pound) whole chicken
2 unpeeled medium lemons (280g), quartered

1   Combine butter, oil, rind, garlic, olives and parsley in medium bowl; season.
2   Rinse chicken under cold water; pat dry, inside and out, with absorbent paper. Use fingers to make a pocket between the breasts and skin; push half the butter mixture under skin. Rub remaining butter mixture all over chicken. Tuck wing tips under chicken; fill cavity with lemon, tie legs together with kitchen string. Trim skin around neck; secure neck flap to underside of chicken with small fine skewers.
3   Place chicken in 4.5-litre (18-cup) slow cooker. Cook, covered, on low, 6 hours.
4   Cut chicken into quarters to serve.

Italian sausages are coarse pork sausages generally sold in plump links. They are usually flavoured with garlic and fennel seed or anise seed, and come in two styles — hot (flavoured with thai red chilli) and sweet (without the added heat). They are available from speciality butchers and delicatessens.

PORK NECK WITH CIDER AND PEAR

1kg (2 pound) piece pork neck
185g (6 ounces) italian pork sausages
1 egg yolk
½ cup (70g) coarsely chopped pistachios
2 tablespoons coarsely chopped fresh sage
1 tablespoon olive oil

1 medium brown onion (150g), quartered
4 cloves garlic, halved
2 medium unpeeled pears (460g), quartered
⅔ cup (160ml) alcoholic apple cider
6 fresh sage leaves

serves 4
prep + cook time
6 hours 30 minutes
nutritional count per serving
45.3g total fat
(13g saturated fat);
3164kJ (757 cal);
19g carbohydrate;
63g protein; 5.6g fibre

Not suitable to freeze.

Serve pork with creamy mashed potato and a radicchio or witlof salad.

1   Place pork on board; slice through thickest part of pork horizontally, without cutting all the way through. Open pork out to form one large piece; trim pork.
2   Squeeze filling from sausages into small bowl, mix in egg yolk, nuts and chopped sage; season. Press sausage mixture along one long side of pork; roll pork to enclose filling. Tie pork with kitchen string at 2.5cm (1 inch) intervals.
3   Heat oil in large frying pan; cook pork, until browned all over. Remove from pan. Add onion and garlic to same pan; cook, stirring, until onion softens.
4   Place pears and onion mixture in 4.5-litre (18-cup) slow cooker; top with pork then add cider and sage leaves. Cook, covered, on low, 6 hours.
5   Serve sliced pork with pear and onion mixture. Sprinkle with extra sage leaves, if you like.

This succulent meltingly tender lamb, flavoured with fresh herbs, garlic and lemon is a classic Greek dish and absolutely delicious.

GREEK-STYLE ROAST LAMB WITH POTATOES

serves 4
prep + cook time
8 hours 40 minutes
nutritional count per serving
29.5g total fat
(10.2g saturated fat);
3206kJ (767 cal);
33.5g carbohydrate;
88.4g protein; 5.6g fibre

Not suitable to freeze. Lamb can be refrigerated, covered, overnight at the end of step 2.

Serve lamb with a greek salad or steamed spinach.

2 tablespoons olive oil
1kg (2 pounds) baby new potatoes
2kg (4 pound) lamb leg
2 sprigs fresh rosemary, chopped coarsely
2 tablespoons finely chopped fresh flat-leaf parsley
2 tablespoons finely chopped fresh oregano
3 cloves garlic, crushed
1 tablespoon finely grated lemon rind
2 tablespoons lemon juice
½ cup (125ml) beef stock

1 Heat half the oil in large frying pan; cook potatoes until browned. Transfer to 4.5-litre (18-cup) slow cooker.
2 Make small cuts in lamb at 2.5cm (1 inch) intervals; press rosemary into cuts. Combine remaining oil, parsley, oregano, garlic, rind and juice in small bowl; rub mixture all over lamb, season.
3 Cook lamb in same heated pan until browned all over. Place lamb on top of potatoes; add stock. Cook, covered, on low, 8 hours.
4 Remove lamb and potatoes; cover lamb, stand 10 minutes before slicing.
5 Serve lamb with potatoes and sauce.

CHAR SIU PORK RIBS

2.5kg (5¼ pounds) american-style pork spare ribs
2 tablespoons peanut oil
½ cup (125ml) char siu sauce
2 tablespoons light soy sauce
¼ cup (60ml) orange juice
5cm (2 inch) piece fresh ginger (25g), grated
2 cloves garlic, crushed
1 fresh long red chilli, chopped finely
2 teaspoons sesame oil

1   Cut rib racks into pieces to fit 4.5-litre (18-cup) slow cooker. Heat peanut oil in large frying pan; cook ribs, in batches, until browned all over.

2   Meanwhile, combine sauces, juice, ginger, garlic, chilli and sesame oil in jug; brush all over ribs. Place ribs in cooker; pour over remaining sauce. Cook, covered, on low, 7 hours.

3   Remove ribs from sauce; cover to keep warm. Place sauce in medium saucepan; bring to the boil. Boil, uncovered, about 5 minutes or until sauce is thickened slightly.

4   Serve ribs drizzled with sauce.

serves 6
prep + cook time
7 hours 25 minutes
nutritional count per serving
23.9g total fat
(6.6g saturated fat);
1760kJ (421 cal);
9.6g carbohydrate;
40.7g protein; 2.7g fibre

Not suitable to freeze.

Serve ribs with steamed rice and stir-fried asian greens.

Ask the butcher to cut the rib racks into pieces that will fit your slow cooker.

Quince is a yellow-skinned fruit
a tart taste. It is commonly cooke
and made into a paste. The long, s
flesh a deep, rose pink. Since anci
been a symbol of love, and everyc

LAMB WITH QUINCE A

1kg (2 pound) piece boneless lamb shoulder
6 cloves garlic, peeled, halved
2 tablespoons finely chopped coriander (cilantro) n
2 teaspoons ground cumin
1 teaspoon ground coriander
1 teaspoon sweet paprika
2 tablespoons olive oil
1 medium brown onion (150g), sliced thickly
1 cup (250ml) chicken stock
1 cinnamon stick
2 tablespoons honey
⅓ cup coarsely chopped fresh coriander (cilantro)
1 tablespoon quince paste

1   Roll and tie lamb with kitchen string at 5cm (2 in
crush garlic, coriander root and stem mixture, spices a
garlic mixture all over lamb; cover, refrigerate 2 hours
2   Heat remaining oil in large frying pan; cook lamb,
Add onion to same pan; cook, stirring, until onion so
3   Place stock, cinnamon and onion mixture in 4.5-li
drizzle with honey. Season with salt and pepper. Cook
10 minutes; stir quince paste into sauce.
4   Thickly slice lamb, serve with sauce; sprinkle with

SLOW-ROASTED CHILLI
AND FENNEL PORK

1kg (2 pound) piece pork shoulder on the bone, rind on
1 medium lemon (140g)
1½ tablespoons fennel seeds
2 teaspoons dried chilli flakes
2 teaspoons sea salt
½ teaspoon cracked black pepper
3 cloves garlic, chopped coarsely
⅓ cup (80ml) olive oil
1 large brown onion (200g), chopped coarsely
½ cup (125ml) chicken stock

1   Using a sharp knife, score pork rind in a criss-cross pattern. Coarsely grate rind from lemon;
chop lemon coarsely.
2   Cook fennel seeds in dry large frying pan until fragrant. Using mortar and pestle, crush seeds.
Add chilli, salt, pepper, garlic, lemon rind and 2 tablespoons of the oil; pound until ground finely.
3   Heat remaining oil in same pan; cook pork, skin-side down, until browned and crisp. Turn
pork; cook until browned all over. Spread fennel mixture all over pork. Place onion, stock and
chopped lemon in 4.5-litre (18-cup) slow cooker; top with pork, skin-side up. Cook, covered,
on low, 7 hours.
4   Remove pork from cooker; stand, covered, 10 minutes before slicing thinly.

serves 6
prep + cook time
7½ hours
nutritional count per serving
24.3g total fat
(6.4g saturated fat);
1384kJ (331 cal);
2.1g carbohydrate;
26.1g protein; 0.7g fibre

Not suitable to freeze.

Serve pork with your
favourite chutney or relish
in crusty bread rolls or
baguettes with a green salad.

Ask the butcher to score the
rind on the pork for you.

CURRIES

RED CURRY LAMB SHANKS

serves 6
prep + cook time
8 hours 40 minutes
nutritional count per serving
33.2g total fat
(18g saturated fat);
2337kJ (559 cal);
17g carbohydrate;
45.6g protein; 6g fibre

Suitable to freeze at the
end of step 2.

Serve with steamed rice.

Snake beans are available
from major supermarkets
and Asian greengrocers. If
you can't find them, use
regular green beans instead.

Red curry paste is available
in various strengths from
supermarkets. Use whichever
one suits your spice-level
tolerance best.

2 tablespoons vegetable oil
6 french-trimmed lamb shanks (2kg)
1 large kumara (orange sweet potato) (500g), chopped coarsely
3 fresh kaffir lime leaves, shredded thinly
1 large brown onion (200g), chopped finely
2 tablespoons red curry paste
1⅔ cups (400ml) canned coconut cream
2 cups (500ml) chicken stock
2 tablespoons fish sauce
375g (12 ounces) snake beans, chopped coarsely
1 cup loosely packed fresh coriander (cilantro) leaves
2 tablespoons lime juice

1   Heat half the oil in large frying pan; cook lamb, in batches, until browned all over. Place lamb in 4.5-litre (18-cup) slow cooker, add kumara and lime leaves.
2   Heat remaining oil in same pan; cook onion, stirring, until soft. Add curry paste; cook, stirring, until fragrant. Add coconut cream; bring to the boil. Remove pan from heat; stir in stock and sauce, pour over lamb. Cook, covered, on low, 8 hours.
3   Add beans to cooker; cook, covered, on high, about 15 minutes. Stir in coriander and juice; season to taste.

CHICKEN, LENTIL AND PUMPKIN CURRY

⅔ cup (130g) dried brown lentils
⅔ cup (130g) dried red lentils
1 tablespoon vegetable oil
1 large brown onion (200g), chopped finely
2 cloves garlic, crushed
2.5cm (1 inch) piece fresh ginger (10g), grated
2 teaspoons ground cumin
2 teaspoons ground coriander
2 teaspoons black mustard seeds
1 teaspoon ground turmeric
1 fresh long red chilli, chopped finely

3 cups (750ml) chicken stock
1kg (2 pounds) chicken thigh fillets,
 chopped coarsely
400g (14½ ounces) canned diced tomatoes
500g (1 pound) pumpkin, chopped coarsely
1¼ cups (270ml) canned coconut milk
155g (5 ounces) baby spinach leaves
½ cup coarsely chopped fresh coriander
 (cilantro)

serves 6
prep + cook time
7 hours 40 minutes
nutritional count per serving
26.3g total fat
(12.8g saturated fat);
2312kJ (553 cal);
27.6g carbohydrate;
47g protein; 10g fibre

Suitable to freeze at the
end of step 2.

Serve curry with chapatis
and plain yogurt.

1 Rinse lentils under cold water until water runs clear; drain.
2 Heat oil in large frying pan; cook onion, garlic and ginger, stirring, until onion softens. Add spices and chilli; cook, stirring, until fragrant. Add stock; bring to the boil.
3 Pour stock mixture into 4.5-litre (18-cup) slow cooker; stir in chicken, undrained tomatoes, pumpkin and lentils. Cook, covered, on low, 7 hours.
4 Stir in coconut milk; cook, covered, on high, 15 minutes, stirring once. Stir in spinach and coriander. Season to taste.

INDIAN VEGETABLE CURRY

serves 6
prep + cook time
5 hours
nutritional count per serving
18.7g total fat
(12.8g saturated fat);
1388kJ (332 cal);
25.4g carbohydrate;
10.7g protein; 10.6g fibre

Suitable to freeze at the
end of step 3.

Serve curry with naan bread
and lemon wedges.

1 tablespoon vegetable oil

1 medium leek (350g), sliced thickly

2 cloves garlic, crushed

2 teaspoons black mustard seeds

2 teaspoons ground cumin

2 teaspoons garam masala

1 teaspoon ground turmeric

1½ cups (375ml) vegetable stock

400g (14½ ounces) canned diced tomatoes

1 large kumara (orange sweet potato) (500g), chopped coarsely

1 large carrot (180g), chopped coarsely

1⅔ cups (400ml) canned coconut milk

375g (12 ounces) brussels sprouts, halved

400g (15 ounces) canned chickpeas (garbanzo beans), rinsed, drained

155g (5 ounces) baby spinach leaves

½ cup coarsely chopped fresh coriander (cilantro)

1 Heat oil in large frying pan; cook leek and garlic, stirring, until leek softens. Add spices; cook, stirring, until fragrant. Add stock; bring to the boil.

2 Pour stock mixture into 4.5-litre (18-cup) slow cooker; stir in undrained tomatoes, kumara, carrot and coconut milk. Cook, covered, on low, 4 hours.

3 Add sprouts and chickpeas to curry. Cook, covered, on high, about 40 minutes or until sprouts are just tender.

4 Stir in spinach and coriander. Season to taste.

Butter chicken is among the best known and most loved Indian food. The silky tomato and butter sauce, infused with various spices, can be made less or more hot accordingly to your taste by reducing or adding the amount of chilli powder.

BUTTER CHICKEN

12 chicken thigh cutlets (2.4kg), skin removed
2 tablespoons lemon juice
1 teaspoon chilli powder
¾ cup (200g) greek-style yogurt
5cm (2 inch) piece fresh ginger (25g), grated
2 teaspoons garam masala
45g (1½ ounces) butter
1 tablespoon vegetable oil
1 medium brown onion (150g), chopped finely
4 cloves garlic, crushed
1 teaspoon ground coriander

1 teaspoon ground cumin
1 teaspoon sweet paprika
2 tablespoons tomato paste
1⅔ cups (410g) canned tomato puree
⅔ cup (160ml) chicken stock
2 tablespoons honey
1 cinnamon stick
⅓ cup (80ml) pouring cream
⅓ cup (80g) ricotta cheese
½ cup loosely packed fresh coriander
  (cilantro) leaves

serves 6
prep + cook time
4 hours 30 minutes
(+ refrigeration)
nutritional count per serving
39.3g total fat
(17g saturated fat);
2750kJ (658 cal);
17.9g carbohydrate;
57.8g protein; 2.6g fibre

Suitable to freeze at the
end of step 3.

Serve with steamed basmati
rice and warm naan bread.

1 Combine chicken, juice and chilli powder in large bowl. Cover, refrigerate 30 minutes.
2 Stir yogurt, ginger and half the garam masala into chicken mixture.
3 Heat butter and oil in large frying pan; cook chicken, in batches, until browned all over. Transfer chicken to 4.5-litre (18-cup) slow cooker. Add onion and garlic to same pan; cook, stirring, until onion softens. Add remaining garam masala and ground spices; cook, stirring, until fragrant. Remove from heat; stir in tomato paste, puree, stock, honey and cinnamon. Transfer tomato mixture to slow cooker. Cook, covered, on low, 4 hours.
4 Stir in cream; season to taste.
5 Serve topped with ricotta and coriander leaves.

CREAMY VEGETABLE AND ALMOND KORMA

serves 6
prep + cook time
6¾ hours
nutritional count per serving
42.8g total fat
(16.2g saturated fat);
2429kJ (581 cal);
29.6g carbohydrate;
14.4g protein; 12.4g fibre

Suitable to freeze at the
end of step 1.

Serve korma with steamed
rice, naan and yogurt.

This is a mild curry. For
more heat, serve curry
sprinkled with some
sliced fresh red chilli.

½ cup (150g) korma paste
½ cup (60g) ground almonds
1 large brown onion (200g), sliced thinly
2 cloves garlic, crushed
½ cup (125ml) vegetable stock
½ cup (125ml) water
300ml (1⅓ cups) pouring cream
375g (12 ounces) baby carrots
125g (4 ounces) baby corn

500g (1 pound) baby potatoes, halved
375g (12 ounces) pumpkin, chopped coarsely
315g (10 ounces) cauliflower, cut into florets
6 medium yellow patty-pan squash (180g),
   halved
½ cup (60g) frozen peas
½ cup (70g) roasted slivered almonds
2 teaspoons black sesame seeds

1   Combine paste, ground almonds, onion, garlic, stock, the water, cream, carrots, corn, potato,
pumpkin and cauliflower in 4.5-litre (18-cup) slow cooker. Cook, covered, on low, 6 hours.
2   Add squash and peas; cook, covered, on high, about 20 minutes. Season to taste. Sprinkle
curry with nuts and seeds.

LAMB ROGAN JOSH

1.5kg (3¼ pounds) boned lamb shoulder, chopped coarsely
2 large brown onions (400g), sliced thinly
5cm (2 inch) piece fresh ginger (25g), grated
3 cloves garlic, crushed
½ cup (150g) rogan josh paste
2 tablespoons tomato paste
400g (14½ ounces) canned diced tomatoes
½ cup (125ml) beef stock
1 cinnamon stick
4 cardamom pods, bruised
2 bay leaves
½ cup loosely packed fresh coriander (cilantro) leaves

1   Combine lamb, onion, ginger, garlic, pastes, undrained tomatoes, stock, cinnamon, cardamom and bay leaves in 4.5-litre (18-cup) slow cooker. Cook, covered, on low, 8 hours. Season to taste.
2   Sprinkle curry with coriander.

serves 6
prep + cook time
8 hours 20 minutes
nutritional count per serving
30.1g total fat
(10.8g saturated fat);
2249kJ (538 cal);
8.8g carbohydrate;
55.7g protein; 5.1g fibre

Suitable to freeze at the end of step 1.

Serve lamb with steamed rice, naan and yogurt.

OLD-FASHIONED CURRIED SAUSAGES

serves 6
prep + cook time
8 hours 20 minutes
nutritional count per serving
79.8g total fat
(37g saturated fat);
4435kJ (1061 cal);
40g carbohydrate;
41.3g protein; 13.7g fibre

Not suitable to freeze.

Serve with crusty bread.

12 thick beef sausages (1.8kg)

1 tablespoon vegetable oil

2 medium brown onions (300g), sliced thinly

2 tablespoons mild curry powder

400g (14½ ounces) canned diced tomatoes

1 cup (250ml) beef stock

1 cup (250ml) water

4 medium potatoes (800g), unpeeled, cut into thick wedges

1 cup (120g) frozen peas, thawed

½ cup (80g) sultanas

1 Place sausages in large saucepan, add enough cold water to cover sausages; bring to the boil. Boil, uncovered, 2 minutes; drain.

2 Heat oil in same pan; cook onion, stirring, until softened. Add curry powder; cook, stirring, until fragrant. Remove from heat; stir in undrained tomatoes, stock and the water.

3 Place potatoes in 4.5-litre (18-cup) slow cooker; top with sausages and onion mixture. Cook, covered, on low, 8 hours.

4 Stir in peas and sultanas. Season to taste.

SPINACH DHAL

500g (1 pound) yellow split peas
45g (1½ ounces) ghee
2 medium brown onions (300g),
  chopped finely
3 cloves garlic, crushed
4cm (1½ inch) piece fresh ginger (20g),
  grated
1 fresh long green chilli, chopped finely
2 tablespoons black mustard seeds
1 teaspoon cumin seeds

1 tablespoon ground coriander
2 teaspoons ground turmeric
1 teaspoon garam masala
800g (28 ounces) canned diced tomatoes
3 cups (750ml) vegetable stock
1½ cups (375ml) water
1 teaspoon caster (superfine) sugar
4 medium silver beet (swiss chard) leaves
  (320g), stems removed, chopped coarsely

serves 6
prep + cook time
10 hours 20 minutes
nutritional count per serving
10.1g total fat
(5.4g saturated fat);
1689kJ (404 cal);
48.2g carbohydrate;
23.3g protein; 12.5g fibre

Suitable to freeze at the
end of step 2.

Serve dhal topped with fried
or caramelised onions.

1   Rinse split peas under cold water until water runs clear; drain.
2   Heat ghee in large frying pan; cook onion, garlic, ginger and chilli, stirring, until
onion softens. Add seeds and spices; cook, stirring, until fragrant. Place onion mixture
into 4.5-litre (18-cup) slow cooker; stir in undrained tomatoes, stock, the water, sugar
and peas. Cook, covered, on low, 10 hours.
3   Stir in silver beet; season to taste.

DUCK VINDALOO

1.8kg (3¾ pound) whole duck
¼ cup (35g) plain (all-purpose) flour
1 tablespoon peanut oil
2 teaspoons cumin seeds
2 teaspoons fenugreek seeds
1 teaspoon ground coriander
1 teaspoon ground turmeric
½ teaspoon ground cardamom
4 fresh small red thai (serrano) chillies, chopped coarsely
3 cloves garlic, quartered

2.5cm (1 inch) piece fresh ginger (15g), sliced thinly
⅓ cup (80ml) white vinegar
½ cup (125ml) chicken stock
1 medium red onion (170g), chopped finely
4 medium potatoes (800g), chopped coarsely
2 tablespoons chicken gravy powder
2 tablespoons water
½ cup loosely packed fresh coriander (cilantro) leaves

serves 6
prep + cook time
6¾ hours
nutritional count per serving
66.5g total fat
(19.6g saturated fat);
3323kJ (795 cal);
22.7g carbohydrate;
26.7g protein; 3g fibre

Not suitable to freeze.

Serve with steamed rice.

This is a mild vindaloo. If you like it hotter, add more fresh chillies when you make the paste.

1 Rinse duck under cold water; pat dry. Cut duck into six serving-sized pieces. Toss duck in flour, shake off excess. Heat oil in large frying pan; cook duck, in batches, until browned. Transfer to 4.5-litre (18-cup) slow cooker.

2 Meanwhile, dry-fry spices in small frying pan until fragrant; cool. Blend or process spices, chilli, garlic, ginger and vinegar until smooth.

3 Stir spice mixture into cooker with stock, onion and potato. Cook, covered, on low, 6 hours. Season to taste.

4 Transfer duck and potato to serving plate. Skim excess fat from sauce. Stir combined gravy powder and the water into sauce in slow cooker. Cook, covered, on high, about 10 minutes or until the sauce thickens.

5 Drizzle sauce over duck; sprinkle with coriander.

DESSERTS

VANILLA AND RED WINE POACHED PEARS

serves 6
prep + cook time
4 hours 50 minutes
(+ cooling)
nutritional count per serving
0.2g total fat
(0g saturated fat);
1225kJ (293 cal);
55.9g carbohydrate;
0.8g protein; 3.3g fibre

Not suitable to freeze.

Serve with whipped cream or vanilla ice-cream.

Store leftover poaching liquid in refrigerator for up to 1 month. Use for poaching more pears or stone fruit.

We used packham pears in this recipe.

6 medium firm pears (1.4kg)
2 cups (500ml) dry red wine
1½ cups (375ml) water
5cm (2 inch) piece orange rind
½ cup (125ml) orange juice
1 cup (220g) caster (superfine) sugar
1 vanilla bean
1 cinnamon stick

1   Peel pears, leaving stems intact.
2   Combine wine, the water, rind, juice and sugar in 4.5-litre (18-cup) slow cooker. Halve vanilla bean lengthways, scrape seeds into slow cooker; add vanilla bean and cinnamon stick.
3   Lay pears down in cooker to cover in wine mixture. Cook, covered, on high, about 4½ hours or until pears are tender. Place 1 cup of the poaching liquid in small saucepan; bring to the boil. Boil, uncovered, about 7 minutes or until syrup is reduced by about half; cool.
4   Meanwhile, place pears in large deep bowl; add remaining poaching liquid, cool.
5   Serve pears drizzled with syrup.

STEAMED CHRISTMAS PUDDING

2½ cups (375g) chopped mixed dried fruit
¾ cup (120g) finely chopped dried
 seedless dates
½ cup (65g) finely chopped dried cranberries
¾ cup (180ml) water
1 cup (220g) firmly packed dark brown sugar
90g (3 ounces) butter, chopped coarsely
1 teaspoon bicarbonate of soda (baking soda)
2 eggs, beaten lightly

¾ cup (110g) plain (all-purpose) flour
¾ cup (110g) self-raising flour
1 teaspoon mixed spice
½ teaspoon ground cinnamon
¼ cup (60ml) dark rum

serves 12
prep + cook time
5½ hours
nutritional count per serving
7.6g total fat
(4.5g saturated fat);
1463kJ (350 cal);
61.5g carbohydrate;
4.1g protein; 3.7g fibre

Suitable to freeze at the end
of step 5; pudding can be
frozen as a whole pudding,
or in serving-sized wedges.

Serve with cream or custard.

The pleated paper and foil
allow space for the pudding
mixture to rise.

1 Combine fruit, the water, sugar and butter in medium saucepan. Stir over heat until butter melts and sugar dissolves; bring to the boil. Reduce heat; simmer, uncovered, 5 minutes. Transfer mixture to large heatproof bowl, stir in soda; cool 10 minutes.
2 Stir eggs, sifted dry ingredients and rum into the fruit mixture.
3 Grease 2-litre (8-cup) pudding steamer; spoon mixture into steamer. Top with pleated baking paper and foil; secure with kitchen string or lid.
4 Place pudding in 4.5-litre (18-cup) slow cooker with enough boiling water to come halfway up side of steamer. Cook, covered, on high, 5 hours, replenishing with boiling water as necessary to maintain level.
5 Remove pudding from cooker, stand 10 minutes before turning onto plate.

Although this pudding has only a few ingredients, it is a labour of love to create. The result is well worth the effort, but keep in mind the time you will need to make it.

MANDARIN AND ALMOND PUDDING

4 small mandarins (mandarin oranges) (400g)
4 eggs
⅔ cup (150g) caster (superfine) sugar
1⅓ cups (160g) ground almonds
⅔ cup (100g) self-raising flour

1   Place washed unpeeled mandarins in 4.5-litre (18-cup) slow cooker; cover with hot water. Cook, covered, on high, 2 hours.
2   Trim ends from mandarins; discard. Halve mandarins; remove and discard seeds. Process mandarins, including rind, until mixture is pulpy.
3   Grease 2-litre (8-cup) pudding steamer.
4   Beat eggs and sugar in small bowl with electric mixer until thick and creamy; fold in ground almonds, sifted flour and mandarin pulp. Spoon mixture into steamer. Top with pleated baking paper and foil; secure with kitchen string or lid.
5   Place pudding in cooker with enough boiling water to come halfway up side of steamer. Cook, covered, on high, 3 hours, replenishing with boiling water as necessary to maintain level. Stand pudding 5 minutes before turning onto plate.

serves 8
prep + cook time
5½ hours
nutritional count per serving
13.9g total fat
(1.6g saturated fat);
1246kJ (298 cal);
32.5g carbohydrate;
9g protein; 3.2g fibre

Not suitable to freeze.

Serve pudding with cream, custard or ice-cream.

The pleated paper and foil simply allow space for the pudding mixture to rise.

This deliciously gooey pudding is a chocolate lover's fantasy. The thick, rich sauce underneath is oozingly chocolately and the pudding is springy and spongy on top.

CHOCOLATE SELF-SAUCING PUDDING

serves 6
prep + cook time
2 hours 50 minutes
nutritional count per serving
15.5g total fat
(9.6g saturated fat);
2424kJ (580 cal);
101.3g carbohydrate;
6.9g protein; 1.6g fibre

Not suitable to freeze.

Serve pudding, hot or warm, dusted with a little sifted icing sugar, and with cream and/or ice-cream.

90g (3 ounces) butter
¾ cup (180ml) milk
1 teaspoon vanilla extract
1 cup (220g) caster (superfine) sugar
1½ cups (225g) self-raising flour
2 tablespoons cocoa powder
1 egg, beaten lightly
1 cup (220g) firmly packed light brown sugar
2 tablespoons cocoa powder, extra
2½ cups (625ml) boiling water

1 Grease 4.5-litre (18-cup) slow cooker bowl.
2 Melt butter in milk over low heat in medium saucepan. Remove from heat; cool 5 minutes. Stir in extract and caster sugar, then sifted flour and cocoa, and egg. Spread mixture into cooker bowl.
3 Sift brown sugar and extra cocoa evenly over mixture; gently pour boiling water evenly over mixture. Cook, covered, on high, about 2½ hours or until centre is firm.
4 Remove bowl from cooker. Stand pudding 5 minutes before serving.

ON THE STOVE TOP

Having a big pot of stew or soup bubbling away on the stove is one of life's true comforts. The rich, flavourful aroma of slow-cooked meat and vegies, with a few herbs and maybe a sprinkling of spices, wafting from the kitchen is instantly calming. It is food for the soul, a reminder that even in our fast-paced hectic lives we still need to take some time out and be soothed by a good old slow-cooked meal. The best type of pot to use is a heavy-based casserole dish or dutch oven, as they will contain and distribute the heat evenly. Make sure the lid fits the dish tightly, or to really seal in the flavours you can cover the dish with a sheet of wet crumpled baking paper and place the lid on top. To ensure you get an even distribution of heat when cooking on the stove, you can use a heat spreading mat, available from supermarkets.

IRISH LAMB AND BARLEY STEW

serves 4
prep + cook time
2 hours
nutritional count per serving
22.6g total fat
(8.2g saturated fat);
2224kJ (532 cal);
37.4g carbohydrate;
40.4g protein; 8.6g fibre

Slow cooker: suitable
to the end of step 2.
Pressure cooker: suitable
to the end of step 3.
Suitable to freeze at the
end of step 2.

2 tablespoons olive oil

1kg (2 pounds) diced lamb shoulder

1 large brown onion (200g), chopped coarsely

2 medium carrots (240g), chopped coarsely

2 stalks celery (300g), trimmed, chopped coarsely

2 cloves garlic, crushed

1 litre (4 cups) chicken stock

2 cups (500ml) water

1 cup (200g) pearl barley

4 sprigs fresh thyme

3 medium potatoes (600g), chopped coarsely

2 cups (160g) finely shredded cabbage

⅓ cup finely chopped fresh flat-leaf parsley

1 Heat half the oil in large saucepan; cook lamb, in batches, until browned. Remove from pan.

2 Heat remaining oil in same pan; cook onion, carrot, celery and garlic, stirring, until vegetables soften. Return lamb to pan with stock, the water, barley and thyme; bring to the boil. Reduce heat; simmer, covered, 1 hour, skimming fat from surface occasionally.

3 Add potato; simmer, uncovered, about 20 minutes or until potato is tender.

4 Add cabbage; simmer, uncovered, until cabbage is just tender. Discard thyme.

5 Serve stew sprinkled with parsley.

BEEF AND PRUNE TAGINE WITH SPINACH COUSCOUS

2 large red onions (600g), chopped finely
2 tablespoons olive oil
1 teaspoon cracked black pepper
pinch saffron threads
1 teaspoon ground cinnamon
¼ teaspoon ground ginger
1kg (2 pounds) beef blade steak, cut into
   4cm (1½ inch) pieces
50g (1½ ounces) butter, chopped
425g (14½ ounces) canned diced tomatoes
1 cup (250ml) water
2 tablespoons white sugar
¾ cup (100g) roasted slivered almonds
1½ cups (250g) seeded prunes
1 teaspoon finely grated lemon rind
¼ teaspoon ground cinnamon, extra

SPINACH COUSCOUS
1½ cups (300g) couscous
1½ cups (375ml) boiling water
80g (3 ounces) finely shredded
   baby spinach leaves

serves 4
prep + cook time
3 hours
nutritional count per serving
50.6g total fat
(16.1g saturated fat);
4861kJ (1163 cal);
99.2g carbohydrate;
72.1g protein; 11.1g fibre

Slow cooker: suitable
to the end of step 2.
Pressure cooker: suitable
to the end of step 2.
Suitable to freeze at the
end of step 2.

1 Combine onion, oil, pepper, saffron, cinnamon and ginger in large bowl, add beef; toss beef to coat in mixture.

2 Place beef in large deep saucepan with butter, undrained tomatoes, the water, half the sugar and ½ cup of the nuts; bring to the boil. Reduce heat; simmer, covered, 1½ hours. Remove 1 cup cooking liquid; reserve. Simmer tagine, uncovered, 30 minutes.

3 Meanwhile, place prunes in small bowl, cover with boiling water; stand 20 minutes, drain. Place prunes in small saucepan with rind, extra cinnamon, remaining sugar and reserved cooking liquid; bring to the boil. Reduce heat; simmer, uncovered, about 15 minutes or until prunes soften. Stir into tagine.

4 Make spinach couscous. Serve couscous with tagine; sprinkle with remaining nuts.

SPINACH COUSCOUS Combine couscous with the water in large heatproof bowl, cover; stand 5 minutes or until water is absorbed, fluffing with fork occasionally. Stir in spinach.

ROGAN JOSH

serves 4
prep + cook time
2½ hours
nutritional count per serving
48.1g total fat
(15.3g saturated fat);
3219kJ (770 cal);
15.7g carbohydrate;
68.9g protein; 5.5g fibre

Slow cooker: not suitable.
Pressure cooker: not suitable.
Not suitable to freeze.

Serve rogan josh with
warmed naan bread.

2 teaspoons ground cardamom
2 teaspoons ground cumin
2 teaspoons ground coriander
1kg (2 pound) boned leg of lamb, trimmed,
  cut into 3cm (1¼ inch) pieces
20g (¾ ounce) butter
2 tablespoons vegetable oil
2 medium brown onions (300g),
  sliced thinly
4cm (1½ inch) piece fresh ginger (20g), grated
4 cloves garlic, crushed
2 teaspoons sweet paprika
½ teaspoon cayenne pepper
½ cup (125ml) beef stock

425g (14½ ounces) canned crushed tomatoes
2 bay leaves
2 cinnamon sticks
¾ cup (200g) yogurt
¾ cup (110g) roasted slivered almonds
1 fresh long red chilli, sliced thinly
CUCUMBER RAITA
1 cup (280g) greek-style yogurt
1 lebanese cucumber (130g) seeded,
  chopped finely
1 tablespoon finely chopped fresh mint

1 Combine cardamom, cumin and coriander in medium bowl, add lamb; toss lamb to coat in spice mixture.

2 Heat butter and half the oil in large deep saucepan; cook lamb, in batches, until browned all over. Remove from pan.

3 Heat remaining oil in same pan; cook onion, ginger, garlic, paprika and cayenne over low heat, stirring, until onion softens.

4 Return lamb to pan with stock, undrained tomatoes, bay leaves and cinnamon. Add yogurt, 1 tablespoon at a time, stirring well between each addition; bring to the boil. Reduce heat; simmer, covered, about 1½ hours or until lamb is tender.

5 Meanwhile, make cucumber raita.

6 Sprinkle lamb with nuts and chilli off the heat; serve with raita.

CUCUMBER RAITA Combine ingredients in small bowl. Season with salt, pepper and ground cumin to taste.

Ancho chillies, the most commonly used chilli in Mexico, are dried poblano chillies. Having a fruity, sweet and smoky flavour with a mild heat, they measure about 8cm in length and are dark reddish brown in colour. They are available from good delicatessens stocking Spanish foods. Use a chopped fresh green chilli if ancho chillies are not available.

MAPLE SYRUP-FLAVOURED PORK BELLY WITH PECANS

serves 4
prep + cook time
2 hours
nutritional count per serving
67.2g total fat
(18.9g saturated fat);
4080kJ (976 cal);
62.3g carbohydrate;
34.7g protein; 4.1g fibre

Slow cooker: suitable
to the end of step 1.
Pressure cooker: suitable
to the end of step 1.
Suitable to freeze at the
end of step 1.

Serve with steamed basmati
and wild rice blend.

1kg (2 pound) piece boned pork belly, cut
  into four pieces
1 cup (250ml) pure maple syrup
3 cups (750ml) chicken stock
1 cinnamon stick
2 ancho chillies
6 whole cloves

2 cloves garlic, crushed
½ cup (125ml) soy sauce
½ cup (125ml) orange juice
1 tablespoon olive oil
750g (1½ pounds) silver beet
  (swiss chard), trimmed, sliced thinly
½ cup (60g) coarsely chopped roasted pecans

1   Combine pork, syrup, stock, cinnamon, chillies, cloves, garlic and sauce in saucepan large enough to hold pork in a single layer; bring to the boil. Reduce heat; simmer, covered, about 1½ hours or until pork is tender, turning pork every 30 minutes.

2   Remove pork from pan; cover to keep warm. Stir juice into braising liquid in pan; bring to the boil. Reduce heat; simmer, uncovered, about 5 minutes or until sauce thickens slightly. Strain sauce into small bowl.

3   Meanwhile, heat oil in large saucepan; cook silver beet, stirring, about 5 minutes or until wilted.

4   Cut each pork piece into quarters. Divide silver beet among plates; top with pork, drizzle with sauce then sprinkle with nuts.

MEXICAN BEANS WITH SAUSAGES

1 cup (200g) dried kidney beans
750g (1½ pounds) beef sausages, chopped coarsely
1 tablespoon olive oil
1 large white onion (200g), chopped coarsely
3 cloves garlic, crushed
1 large red capsicum (bell pepper) (350g), chopped coarsely
½ teaspoon ground cumin
2 teaspoons sweet smoked paprika
1 teaspoon dried chilli flakes
800g (28 ounces) canned crushed tomatoes
2 tablespoons coarsely chopped fresh oregano

serves 4
prep + cook time
2½ hours
(+ standing)
nutritional count per serving
56.9g total fat
(25.2g saturated fat);
3323kJ (795 cal);
33.5g carbohydrate;
38.1g protein; 20.2g fibre

Slow cooker: not suitable.
Pressure cooker: not suitable.
Suitable to freeze at the end
of step 4.

Serve with warmed tortillas.

1 Place beans in medium bowl, cover with cold water; stand overnight, drain. Rinse under cold water; drain. Place beans in medium saucepan of boiling water; return to the boil. Reduce heat; simmer, uncovered, about 30 minutes or until beans are almost tender. Drain.
2 Cook sausages, in batches, in heated large deep saucepan until browned; drain on absorbent paper.
3 Heat oil in same pan; cook onion, garlic and capsicum, stirring, until onion softens. Add cumin, paprika and chilli; cook, stirring, about 2 minutes or until fragrant. Add beans and undrained tomatoes; bring to the boil. Reduce heat; simmer, covered, about 1 hour or until beans are tender.
4 Return sausages to pan; simmer, covered, about 10 minutes or until sausages are cooked through. Remove from heat; stir in oregano.

LAMB, APRICOT AND ALMOND TAGINE

serves 4
prep + cook time
2 hours
nutritional count per serving
41.7g total fat
(12.1g saturated fat);
3018kJ (722 cal);
22.1g carbohydrate;
61.3g protein; 7.8g fibre

Slow cooker: suitable
to the end of step 3.
Pressure cooker: suitable
to the end of step 3.
Suitable to freeze at the
end of step 3.

2 tablespoons olive oil
1kg (2 pounds) diced lamb
12 shallots (300g), halved
1 medium red capsicum (bell pepper)
  (200g), chopped coarsely
2 cloves garlic, crushed
2cm (¾ inch) piece fresh ginger (10g), grated
1 teaspoon ground cumin
1½ cups (375ml) water

1½ cups (375ml) chicken stock
½ teaspoon saffron threads
1 cup (150g) dried apricots halves
1 tablespoon finely chopped
  preserved lemon rind
200g (7 ounces) green beans, trimmed,
  chopped coarsely
½ cup (70g) slivered almonds

1   Heat half the oil in large saucepan; cook lamb, in batches, until browned. Remove from pan.
2   Heat remaining oil in same pan; cook shallot, capsicum, garlic, ginger and cumin, stirring, until fragrant.
3   Return lamb to pan; add the water, stock and saffron, bring to the boil. Reduce heat; simmer, covered, about 1 hour or until lamb is tender.
4   Add apricots, rind and beans; simmer, uncovered, 15 minutes.
5   Serve tagine sprinkled with nuts.

TOMATO-BRAISED LAMB SHANKS

1 tablespoon olive oil
4 french-trimmed lamb shanks (1kg)
1 medium brown onion (150g), sliced thinly
2 medium carrots (240g), chopped finely
2 stalks celery (300g), trimmed, sliced thinly
2 cloves garlic, crushed

½ cup (125ml) dry red wine
1¾ cups (430ml) beef stock
4 medium tomatoes (600g), chopped coarsely
410g (14½ ounces) canned crushed tomatoes
2 tablespoons tomato paste
4 sprigs fresh thyme

serves 4
prep + cook time
2½ hours
nutritional count per serving
7.7g total fat
(1.9g saturated fat);
1250kJ (299 cal);
13.2g carbohydrate;
35.2g protein; 6.8g fibre

Slow cooker: suitable
to the end of recipe.
Pressure cooker: suitable
to the end of recipe.
Suitable to freeze at the
end of recipe.

1   Heat oil in large saucepan; cook lamb, in batches, until browned. Remove from pan.
2   Cook onion, carrot, celery and garlic in same heated pan, stirring, until celery softens.
3   Return lamb to pan with wine, stock, fresh and undrained tomatoes, paste and thyme;
bring to the boil. Reduce heat; simmer, covered, 1 hour, stirring occasionally. Uncover; simmer
about 1 hour or until lamb is tender.

PERSIAN LAMB AND RHUBARB STEW

serves 4
prep + cook time
2½ hours
nutritional count per serving
26g total fat
(14.1g saturated fat);
3319kJ (794 cal);
70.1g carbohydrate;
66.3g protein; 5.1g fibre

Slow cooker: suitable
to the end of step 2.
Pressure cooker: suitable
to the end of step 2.
Suitable to freeze at the
end of step 2.

Make sure the rhubarb you
use is a rich, strong red
colour, otherwise the flavour
of the finished stew will be
too tart. Frozen rhubarb can
be used instead of fresh.

40g (1½ ounces) butter

1kg (2 pounds) diced lamb

1 medium brown onion (150g), sliced thinly

¼ teaspoon saffron threads

½ teaspoon ground cinnamon

¼ teaspoon ground turmeric

1 cup (250ml) water

2 cups (500ml) chicken stock

2 tablespoons tomato paste

2 ¾ cups (300g) coarsely chopped rhubarb

¼ cup finely chopped fresh mint

OLIVE AND PARSLEY COUSCOUS

1½ cups (375ml) vegetable stock

1½ cups (300g) couscous

30g (1 ounce) butter

1 cup seeded kalamata olives

½ cup coarsely chopped fresh flat-leaf parsley

1 Melt half the butter in large deep saucepan; cook lamb, in batches, until browned all over. Remove from pan.
2 Melt remaining butter in same heated pan; cook onion, stirring, until soft. Add spices; cook, stirring, until fragrant. Add the water, stock and paste; bring to the boil. Return lamb to pan; simmer, covered, 1 hour 20 minutes, stirring occasionally.
3 Uncover; simmer about 20 minutes or until lamb is tender. Add rhubarb to pan; simmer, uncovered, about 10 minutes or until rhubarb has softened.
4 Meanwhile, make olive and parsley couscous.
5 Stir mint into stew off the heat; serve stew with couscous.

OLIVE AND PARSLEY COUSCOUS Bring stock to the boil in medium saucepan. Remove from heat; stir in couscous and butter. Cover; stand about 5 minutes or until liquid is absorbed, fluffing with fork occasionally. Stir in olives and parsley.

LAMB AND OKRA IN RICH TOMATO SAUCE WITH GARLIC CONFIT

serves 4
prep + cook time
2½ hours
nutritional count per serving
33.5g total fat
(15g saturated fat);
2286kJ (547 cal);
8g carbohydrate;
53.4g protein; 6.4g fibre

Slow cooker: suitable
to the end of step 2.
Pressure cooker: suitable
to the end of step 2.
Suitable to freeze at the
end of step 2.

Serve with steamed white
long-grain rice.

1 tablespoon olive oil

1kg (2 pounds) boned lamb shoulder, trimmed, chopped coarsely

2 medium brown onions (300g), chopped coarsely

7 medium tomatoes (1kg), chopped coarsely

1 litre (4 cups) water

200g (7 ounces) okra

½ cup loosely packed fresh mint leaves

GARLIC CONFIT

1 teaspoon coriander seeds

½ teaspoon cardamom seeds

30g (1 ounce) butter

5 cloves garlic, sliced thinly

1 teaspoon dried chilli flakes

1 teaspoon salt

1 Heat oil in large deep saucepan; cook lamb, in batches, until browned all over. Remove from pan.

2 Cook onion in same heated pan, stirring, until soft. Add tomato and the water; bring to the boil. Return lamb to pan, reduce heat; simmer, uncovered, stirring occasionally, about 1¾ hours or until lamb is tender.

3 Add okra to lamb mixture; simmer, uncovered, 15 minutes or until okra is tender.

4 Meanwhile, make garlic confit.

5 Serve casserole with garlic confit; sprinkle with mint.

GARLIC CONFIT Using mortar and pestle, crush seeds. Melt butter in small saucepan; cook seeds, garlic, chilli and salt, stirring, over low heat, 10 minutes or until garlic softens.

IN THE OVEN

There's something wonderfully satisfying about the moment you close the oven door and leave a casserole to slowly simmer away. You've done the all the work and now you can leave it to cook itself and develop its rich flavours. As with slow-cooking on the stove, it is best to use a heavy-based pot such as a dutch oven or casserole dish that will hold and radiate the oven's heat evenly throughout the pot. When using cheaper cuts of meat, like chuck or blade steak, you should remove the excess fat and the large pieces of gristle, but the smaller connective tissue will break down and help thicken and flavour the sauce. When dicing the meat you should cut it against the grain where possible, and browning it first is the key to giving the sauce more flavour and making it a rich, brown colour.

VEAL WITH ARTICHOKES, OLIVES AND LEMON

1 medium unpeeled lemon (140g),
  chopped coarsely
4 medium globe artichokes (800g)
1.2kg (2½ pounds) diced veal neck
¼ cup (35g) plain (all-purpose) flour
50g (1½ ounces) butter
¼ cup (60ml) olive oil
1 medium brown onion (150g),
  chopped finely
1 medium carrot (120g), chopped finely

2 cloves garlic, chopped finely
2 sprigs fresh marjoram
2 sprigs fresh oregano
1 cup (250ml) dry white wine
2 cups (500ml) chicken stock
1 cup (150g) seeded kalamata olives
2 teaspoons finely grated lemon rind
2 tablespoons lemon juice
2 tablespoons fresh oregano leaves
1 medium lemon (140g), cut into wedges

serves 6
prep + cook time
3 hours
nutritional count per serving
21.6g total fat
(7.4g saturated fat);
2040kJ (488 cal);
14.6g carbohydrate;
50.2g protein; 3.4g fibre

Slow cooker: suitable
to the end of step 5.
Pressure cooker: suitable
to the end of step 4.
Suitable to freeze at the
end of step 4.

Serve with penne pasta.

1   Place chopped lemon in large bowl half-filled with cold water. Discard outer leaves from artichokes; cut tips from remaining leaves. Trim then peel stalks. Quarter artichokes lengthways; using teaspoon, remove and discard chokes. Place artichokes into the lemon water.
2   Preheat oven to 140°C/280°F.
3   Coat veal in flour; shake off excess. Heat butter and 2 tablespoons of the oil in large flameproof casserole dish on stove top; cook veal, in batches, until browned. Remove from dish.
4   Heat remaining oil in same dish; cook onion, carrot, garlic, marjoram and oregano sprigs, stirring, until vegetables soften. Add wine; bring to the boil. Return veal to dish with stock; cover. Transfer to oven; cook 1 hour.
5   Add artichokes, cover; return to oven, cook 30 minutes. Uncover; cook about 30 minutes or until veal is tender.
6   Stir in olives, rind and juice. Divide among serving plates; top with oregano leaves. Serve with lemon wedges.

Many people are scared of using anchovies because they find them too fishy and don't like the texture. However, when they are cooked, they melt into the other ingredients and add a wonderful earthy saltiness to the dish, and you'd never pick that anchovies were in it.

ANCHOVY AND CHILLI LAMB NECK CHOPS WITH CREAMY POLENTA

serves 4
prep + cook time
3 hours (+ refrigeration)
nutritional count per serving
43.1g total fat
(19.4g saturated fat);
3791kJ (907 cal);
45g carbohydrate;
79.9g protein; 3.9g fibre

Slow cooker: suitable
to the end of step 5.
Pressure cooker: suitable
to the end of step 4.
Suitable to freeze at the
end of step 5.

4 drained anchovy fillets, chopped finely
2 fresh small red thai (seranno) chillies,
  chopped finely
4 cloves garlic, crushed
½ cup (125ml) dry red wine
8 lamb neck chops (1.4kg), trimmed
2 tablespoons olive oil
1 medium brown onion (150g),
  chopped coarsely
1 tablespoon plain (all-purpose) flour
400g (14½ ounces) canned crushed tomatoes
2 cups (500ml) beef stock

CREAMY POLENTA
2 cups (500ml) milk
2 cups (500ml) water
1 cup (170g) polenta
½ cup (40g) finely grated parmesan cheese
½ cup (125ml) pouring cream
½ cup coarsely chopped fresh flat-leaf parsley

1   Combine anchovy, chilli, garlic and wine in medium bowl, add lamb; turn lamb to coat in marinade. Cover; refrigerate 3 hours or overnight.
2   Preheat oven to 140°C/280°F.
3   Heat half the oil in deep medium baking dish on stove top; cook undrained lamb, in batches, until browned all over. Remove from dish. Heat remaining oil in same dish; cook onion, stirring, until softened. Add flour; cook, stirring, about 5 minutes or until flour mixture browns lightly.
4   Return lamb to dish with undrained tomatoes and stock; cover. Transfer to oven; cook 1½ hours.
5   Uncover, skim fat from surface, return to oven; cook, uncovered, turning lamb occasionally, about 30 minutes or until lamb is tender.
6   Meanwhile, make creamy polenta.
7   Divide polenta among serving plates, top with lamb; sprinkle with extra coarsely chopped fresh flat-leaf parsley to serve.

CREAMY POLENTA   Combine milk and the water in large saucepan; bring to the boil. Gradually add polenta to liquid, stirring constantly. Reduce heat; simmer, stirring, about 5 minutes or until polenta thickens. Stir in cheese, cream and parsley.

LEG OF LAMB ON LEMON SCENTED POTATOES

serves 6
prep + cook time
1¾ hours
nutritional count per serving
12.4g total fat
(6.1g saturated fat);
1547kJ (370 cal);
23.3g carbohydrate;
39.3g protein; 3.3g fibre

Slow cooker: suitable
to the end of step 5.
Pressure cooker: not suitable.
Not suitable to freeze.

4 slices pancetta (60g), chopped finely
2 cloves garlic, crushed
1 tablespoon finely chopped fresh rosemary
1 tablespoon finely grated lemon rind
1.2kg (2½ pound) easy-carve leg of lamb
6 medium potatoes (1.2kg), sliced thinly
¼ cup (60ml) lemon juice
1 cup (250ml) chicken stock
25g (¾ ounces) butter, chopped coarsely
1 medium lemon (140g), cut into wedges

1   Preheat oven to 220°C/400°F.
2   Combine pancetta, garlic, rosemary and rind in small bowl.
3   Using sharp knife, pierce lamb all over; press pancetta mixture into cuts.
4   Place potato in large baking dish; drizzle with juice and stock, dot with butter.
5   Place lamb on potato; roast, uncovered, 20 minutes. Reduce oven temperature to
180°C/325°F; roast about 1 hour or until lamb is cooked as desired.
6   Cover lamb; stand 10 minutes before slicing. Serve lamb with potatoes and lemon wedges.

LAMB SHANKS BOURGUIGNON

12 baby onions (300g)
8 french-trimmed lamb shanks (2kg)
¼ cup (35g) plain (all-purpose) flour
1 tablespoon olive oil
20g (¾ ounce) butter
6 rindless bacon slices (390g), chopped coarsely
300g (10 ounces) button mushrooms

2 cloves garlic, crushed
1 cup (250ml) dry red wine
1 cup (250ml) beef stock
1 cup (250ml) water
2 tablespoons tomato paste
2 bay leaves
1 tablespoon light brown sugar

serves 4
prep + cook time
2½ hours
nutritional count per serving
37.5g total fat
(15.2g saturated fat);
3248kJ (777 cal);
15.5g carbohydrate;
82.3g protein; 3.8g fibre

Slow cooker: suitable
to the end of step 6.
Pressure cooker: suitable
to the end of step 5.
Not suitable to freeze.

Serve with mashed potatoes.

1 Preheat oven to 180°C/325°F.
2 Peel onions, leaving root ends intact.
3 Coat lamb in flour; shake off excess. Heat oil in large flameproof casserole dish on stove top; cook lamb, in batches, until browned. Remove from dish.
4 Melt butter in same heated dish; cook onions, bacon, mushrooms and garlic, stirring, until vegetables are browned lightly.
5 Return lamb to dish with wine, stock, the water, paste, bay leaves and sugar; bring to the boil. Cover dish; transfer to oven. Cook 1½ hours.
6 Uncover; cook in oven about 30 minutes or until lamb is tender and sauce thickens slightly.
7 Divide lamb among serving bowls; drizzle with sauce.

Braising is a cooking technique that is usually used for tougher, less expensive cuts of meat. The meat is seared, or browned, and then simmered in liquid on a low heat in a covered pot. The resulting meat is beautifully tender and flavourful.

BRAISED LEG OF LAMB WITH BEANS

serves 6
prep + cook time
2½ hours (+ standing)
nutritional count per serving
35.8g total fat
(16.4g saturated fat);
2872kJ (687 cal);
32.2g carbohydrate;
49.6g protein; 6.2g fibre

Slow cooker: suitable to the end of step 6.
Pressure cooker: suitable to the end of step 6.
Suitable to freeze at the end of step 7.

1 cup (200g) dried borlotti beans
6 cloves garlic, crushed
1 tablespoon coarsely chopped fresh rosemary
2 teaspoons sea salt
1 teaspoon cracked black pepper
¼ cup (60ml) olive oil
1.5kg (3¾ pound) butterflied leg of lamb
2 medium brown onions (300g), chopped coarsely
2 medium carrots (240g), chopped coarsely

2 stalks celery (300g), trimmed, chopped coarsely
2 bay leaves
2 sprigs fresh rosemary
1 cup (250ml) dry white wine
2 cups (500ml) chicken stock
MASHED POTATOES
4 medium potatoes (800g), chopped coarsely
50g (1½ ounces) softened butter
½ cup (125ml) hot pouring cream

1 Place beans in medium bowl, cover with cold water; stand overnight, drain. Rinse under cold water; drain. Cook beans in medium saucepan of boiling water, uncovered, about 15 minutes or until beans are just tender; drain.

2 Preheat oven to 140°C/280°F.

3 Combine garlic, chopped rosemary, salt, pepper and 1 tablespoon of the oil in small bowl. Place lamb, cut-side up, on board; rub garlic mixture into lamb. Roll lamb tightly; secure at 2cm (¾ inch) intervals with kitchen string.

4 Heat remaining oil in large deep flameproof baking dish on stove top; cook lamb until browned all over. Remove lamb from dish.

5 Cook onion, carrot and celery in same heated dish, stirring, until onion softens. Add beans, bay leaves, rosemary sprigs, wine and stock to dish; bring to the boil.

6 Return lamb to dish, cover; transfer to oven, cook 1 hour.

7 Uncover; cook in oven 30 minutes. Discard herbs; remove lamb from dish. Cover lamb; stand 10 minutes, then slice thickly.

8 Meanwhile, make mashed potatoes. Serve lamb on vegetable mixture, accompanied with mashed potatoes.

MASHED POTATOES Boil, steam or microwave potatoes until tender; drain. Mash potato with butter and cream until smooth.

This recipe is very similar to the classic Greek dish moussaka, but the addition of the polenta topping gives it a lovely crust and makes it even more hearty and comforting.

BEEF AND EGGPLANT BAKE WITH POLENTA CRUST

serves 6
prep + cook time
1¾ hours (+ standing)
nutritional count per serving
19.9g total fat
(8.7g saturated fat);
1877kJ (449 cal);
32g carbohydrate;
32.3g protein; 4.7g fibre

Slow cooker: suitable
to the end of step 2.
Pressure cooker: suitable
to the end of step 2.
Suitable to freeze at the
end of the recipe.

Serve with a mixed green
leafy salad.

2 medium eggplants (600g), sliced thickly
2 tablespoons coarse cooking (kosher) salt
1 tablespoon olive oil
1 medium brown onion (150g),
  chopped coarsely
1 medium red capsicum (bell pepper)
  (200g), chopped coarsely
1 clove garlic, crushed
500g (1 pound) minced (ground) beef
2 tablespoons tomato paste
½ cup (125ml) dry red wine

400g (14½ ounces) canned whole tomatoes
1 cup firmly packed fresh basil leaves
1 tablespoon fresh oregano leaves
2 cups (500ml) chicken stock
2 cups (500ml) milk
1 cup (170g) polenta
1½ cups (150g) coarsely grated
  mozzarella cheese

1 Place eggplant in colander, sprinkle all over with salt; stand 30 minutes. Rinse eggplant; drain on absorbent paper.
2 Meanwhile, heat oil in medium frying pan; cook onion, capsicum and garlic, stirring, until onion softens. Add beef; cook, stirring, until beef changes colour. Add paste; cook, stirring, 2 minutes. Add wine; cook, stirring, 5 minutes. Add undrained tomatoes; bring to the boil. Reduce heat; simmer, uncovered, stirring occasionally, about 15 minutes or until liquid is almost evaporated. Coarsely chop about a quarter of the basil leaves; stir into sauce with oregano.
3 Preheat oven to 180°C/350°F.
4 Cook eggplant on heated oiled grill plate (or grill or broiler) until just browned.
5 Meanwhile, combine stock and milk in medium saucepan; bring to the boil. Gradually add polenta, stirring constantly. Simmer, stirring, about 10 minutes or until polenta thickens.
6 Arrange half of the eggplant in shallow 3-litre (12-cup) baking dish; top with half of the beef mixture. Top with remaining eggplant then remaining beef mixture and remaining basil. Spread polenta over basil; sprinkle with cheese. Cook, uncovered, in oven, about 20 minutes or until top is browned lightly. Stand 10 minutes before serving.

BEEF STEW WITH PARSLEY DUMPLINGS

1kg (2 pounds) beef chuck steak, diced into
  5cm (2 inch) pieces
2 tablespoons plain (all-purpose) flour
2 tablespoons olive oil
20g (¾ ounce) butter
2 medium brown onions (300g),
  chopped coarsely
2 cloves garlic, crushed
2 medium carrots (240g), chopped coarsely
1 cup (250ml) dry red wine
2 tablespoons tomato paste
2 cups (500ml) beef stock
4 sprigs fresh thyme

PARSLEY DUMPLINGS
1 cup (150g) self-raising flour
50g (1½ ounces) butter
1 egg, beaten lightly
¼ cup (20g) coarsely grated parmesan cheese
¼ cup finely chopped fresh flat-leaf parsley
⅓ cup (50g) drained sun-dried tomatoes,
  chopped finely
¼ cup (60ml) milk, approximately

serves 4
prep + cook time
3 hours
nutritional count per serving
39.7g total fat
(17.4g saturated fat);
3457kJ (827 cal);
43g carbohydrate;
63.9g protein; 6.7g fibre

Slow cooker: suitable
to the end of step 3.
Pressure cooker: suitable
to the end of step 3.
Suitable to freeze at the
end of step 3.

Serve stew with a mixed
green leafy salad dressed
with a vinaigrette.

1 Preheat oven to 160°C/325°F.
2 Coat beef in flour; shake off excess. Heat oil in large flameproof casserole dish on the stove top;
cook beef, in batches, until browned all over. Remove from dish.
3 Melt butter in same heated dish; cook onion, garlic and carrot, stirring, until vegetables soften.
Add wine; cook, stirring, until liquid reduces to ¼ cup. Return beef to dish with paste, stock and
thyme; bring to the boil. Cover, transfer to oven; cook 1¾ hours.
4 Meanwhile, make parsley dumpling mixture.
5 Remove dish from oven; drop level tablespoons of the dumpling mixture, about 2cm (¾ inch)
apart, onto top of stew. Cook, uncovered, in oven, about 20 minutes or until dumplings are
browned lightly and cooked through.

PARSLEY DUMPLINGS Place flour in medium bowl; rub in butter. Stir in egg, cheese, parsley,
tomato and enough milk to make a soft, sticky dough.

Barley is a wonderful, healthy and tasty way to thicken soups and stews. The barley used in cooking is pearl barley, which is made by husking, steaming and polishing the grains, similarly to white rice. It has a mild, nutty flavour and a low glycemic index rating, which means it will give you energy for longer.

BEEF, BARLEY AND MUSHROOM STEW WITH PARSNIP MASH

serves 4
prep + cook time
3 hours
nutritional count per serving
36.3g total fat
(15.6g saturated fat);
3570kJ (854 cal);
53.6g carbohydrate;
66.1g protein; 14g fibre

Slow cooker: suitable
to the end of step 4.
Pressure cooker: suitable
to the end of step 3.
Suitable to freeze at the
end of step 3.

1kg (2 pounds) beef chuck steak, diced into 3cm pieces
¼ cup (35g) plain (all-purpose) flour
2 tablespoons olive oil
20g (¾ ounce) butter
2 medium brown onions (300g), chopped finely
3 cloves garlic, crushed
1 medium carrot (120g), chopped finely
1 stalk celery (150g), trimmed, chopped finely
4 sprigs fresh thyme
1 sprig fresh rosemary
1 bay leaf

½ cup (100g) pearl barley
2 cups (500ml) beef stock
½ cup (125ml) dry white wine
2 cups (500ml) water
200g (7 ounces) swiss brown mushrooms, quartered
200g (7 ounces) button mushrooms, quartered
PARSNIP MASH
4 medium parsnips (1kg), coarsely chopped
¾ cup (180ml) hot milk
2 cloves garlic, crushed
40g (1¼ ounces) butter, softened

1 Preheat oven to 140°C/280°F.
2 Coat beef in flour; shake off excess. Heat oil in large flameproof casserole dish on stove top; cook beef, in batches, until browned all over. Remove from dish.
3 Melt butter in same heated dish; cook onion, garlic, carrot, celery and herbs, stirring, until vegetables soften. Add barley, stock, wine and the water; bring to the boil. Return beef to dish, cover; cook in oven 1½ hours.
4 Stir in mushrooms; cook, uncovered, in oven, about 30 minutes or until beef and mushrooms are tender.
5 Meanwhile, make parsnip mash.
6 Serve stew with mash; sprinkle with fresh thyme, if you like.

PARSNIP MASH Boil, steam or microwave parsnip until tender; drain. Mash parsnip with milk until smooth; stir in garlic and butter.

SLOW-ROASTED DUCK
WITH BALSAMIC-GLAZ

4 duck marylands (1.2kg), trimmed
2 teaspoons sea salt
2 medium potatoes (400g), chopped coarsely
2 medium carrots (240g), chopped coarsely
2 medium parsnips (460g), chopped coarsely

¼
20
½
f
⅓

1 Preheat oven to 180°C/325°F.
2 Rub skin of duck with sea salt.
3 Combine vegetables, vinegar and butter in large sh
in single layer. Place duck, skin-side up, on top of veget
4 Increase oven temperature to 220°C/400°F; roast a
crisp and vegetables are glazed.
5 Toss parsley and nuts with vegetables in baking dish

SLOW-COOKED DUCK
WITH CABBAGE AND FEN

serves 4
prep + cook time
2¾ hours
nutritional count per serving
61.7g total fat
(20.5g saturated fat);
3783kJ (905 cal);
50.3g carbohydrate;
31.5g protein; 14.5g fibre

Slow cooker: suitable
to the end of step 2.
Pressure cooker: suitable
to the end of step 2.
Not suitable to freeze.

½ small red cabbage (600g), cut into
    four wedges
1 large leek (500g), chopped coarsely
4 baby fennel bulbs (520g), trimmed,
    halved lengthways
1 tablespoon fresh rosemary leaves
2 cloves garlic, sliced thinly
1 cup (250ml) chicken stock

1 Preheat oven to 140°C/280°F.
2 Combine cabbage, leek, fennel, rosemary, gar
dish. Rub duck skin with salt; place duck, skin-sid
about 2¼ hours or until duck meat is tender an
3 Meanwhile, make balsamic-roasted potatoes
4 Strain pan juices through muslin-lined sieve
mixture to keep warm. Skim fat from surface o
about 5 minutes or until sauce thickens slightly
5 Serve duck with cabbage mixture and balsam

BALSAMIC-ROASTED POTATOES Combine po
Roast, uncovered, alongside duck, about 1¼ h
lightly, brushing potatoes occasionally with vir

BRAISED SWEET GINGER DUCK

serves 4
prep + cook time
2 hours
nutritional count per serving
105.7g total fat
(31.7g saturated fat);
4974kJ (1190 cal);
17.9g carbohydrate;
40.8g protein; 3.5g fibre

Slow cooker: not suitable.
Pressure cooker: not suitable.
Not suitable to freeze.

Serve with steamed rice.

1.8kg (3¾ pound) whole duck
3 cups (750ml) water
½ cup (125ml) chinese cooking wine
⅓ cup (80ml) japanese soy sauce
¼ cup (55g) firmly packed light brown sugar
1 whole star anise
3 green onions (scallions), halved
3 cloves garlic, quartered
10cm (4 inch) piece fresh ginger (50g), unpeeled, chopped coarsely
2 teaspoons sea salt
1 teaspoon five-spice powder
750g (1½ pounds) baby buk choy, halved

1 Preheat oven to 160°C/325°F.
2 Discard neck from duck, wash duck; pat dry, inside and out, with absorbent paper. Score duck
in thickest parts of skin; cut duck in half through breastbone and along both sides of backbone,
discard backbone. Tuck wings under duck.
3 Place duck, skin-side down, in medium shallow baking dish; add the combined water, cooking
wine, sauce, sugar, star anise, onion, garlic and ginger. Cover; cook, in oven, about 1 hour or until
duck is cooked through.
4 Increase oven temperature to 200°C/400°F. Remove duck from braising liquid in pan; strain
liquid through muslin-lined sieve into large saucepan. Place duck, skin-side up, on wire rack in same
baking dish. Rub combined salt and five-spice all over duck; roast duck, uncovered, in oven about
30 minutes or until skin is crisp.
5 Discard fat from surface of braising liquid; bring to the boil. Reduce heat; simmer, uncovered,
10 minutes. Add buk choy; simmer, covered, about 5 minutes or until buk choy is just tender.
6 Cut duck halves into two pieces; divide buk choy, braising liquid and duck among serving plates.

CHICKEN AND MERGUEZ CASSOULET

1½ cups (290g) dried lima beans
1 tablespoon vegetable oil
8 chicken thigh cutlets (1.3kg), halved
6 merguez sausages (480g)
1 large brown onion (200g), chopped coarsely
2 medium carrots (240g), cut into
  1cm (½ inch) pieces
2 cloves garlic, chopped finely
4 sprigs fresh thyme
2 tablespoons tomato paste
1 teaspoon finely grated lemon rind

425g (14½ ounces) canned diced tomatoes
1 cup (250ml) chicken stock
1 cup (250ml) water
2 cups (140g) fresh breadcrumbs
GREEN ONION COUSCOUS
2 cups (500ml) chicken stock
2 cups (400g) couscous
30g (1 ounce) butter
2 green onions (scallions), sliced thinly

serves 4
prep + cook time
3¼ hours (+ standing)
nutritional count per serving
66.8g total fat
(23.5g saturated fat);
5267kJ (1260 cal);
65.6g carbohydrate;
90.7g protein; 19.3g fibre

Slow cooker: suitable
to the end of step 5.
Pressure cooker: suitable
to the end of step 4.
Suitable to freeze at the
end of step 4.

Ask your butcher to halve
the chicken thigh cutlets.

You can also brown the
cassoulet in the oven;
place it, uncovered, in a
180°C/350°F oven, about
10 minutes or until the
breadcrumbs brown lightly.

1 Place beans in medium bowl, cover with cold water; stand overnight, drain. Rinse under cold water; drain. Cook beans in large saucepan of boiling water, uncovered, 10 minutes; drain.

2 Heat oil in large flameproof casserole dish on stove top; cook chicken, in batches, until browned all over. Remove from dish. Cook sausages, in batches, in same heated dish until browned all over. Drain on absorbent paper; halve sausages. Reserve 1 tablespoon of fat from dish; discard remainder.

3 Preheat oven to 140°C/280°F.

4 Heat reserved fat in same dish on stove top; cook onion, carrot, garlic and thyme, stirring, until onion softens. Add paste; cook, stirring, 2 minutes. Return chicken to dish with drained beans, rind, undrained tomatoes, stock and the water; bring to the boil. Cover, transfer to oven; cook 40 minutes.

5 Uncover; cook, in oven, about 1¼ hours or until liquid is almost absorbed and beans are tender.

6 Preheat grill (broiler). Sprinkle cassoulet with breadcrumbs; place under grill until breadcrumbs are browned lightly.

7 Meanwhile, make green onion couscous. Serve cassoulet with couscous.

GREEN ONION COUSCOUS Place stock in medium saucepan; bring to the boil. Remove from heat, stir in couscous and butter, cover; stand about 5 minutes or until stock is absorbed, fluffing with fork occasionally. Add onion; toss gently to combine.

Chipotle chillies, also known as ahumado, are jalapeño chillies that have been dried then smoked. They are about 6cm in length, a dark brown, almost black, colour and have a deep, intense smoky flavour rather than a blast of heat. They are available from herb and spice shops and gourmet delicatessens.

CHIPOTLE PORK RIBS WITH CHORIZO AND SMOKED PAPRIKA

serves 4
prep + cook time
3 hours
nutritional count per serving
101.8g total fat
(32.1g saturated fat);
6012kJ (1438 cal);
45.2g carbohydrate;
80.1g protein; 15.7g fibre

Slow cooker: suitable
to the end of step 5.
Pressure cooker: suitable
to the end of step 5.
Suitable to freeze at the
end of step 5.

Serve with flour tortillas.

4 chipotle chillies
1 cup (250ml) boiling water
1.5kg (3¼ pounds) pork belly ribs
1 tablespoon olive oil
1 chorizo sausage (170g), sliced thinly
2 medium red onions (340g), chopped coarsely
1 medium red capsicum (bell pepper)
  (200g), chopped coarsely
1 medium green capsicum (bell pepper)
  (200g), chopped coarsely
1 teaspoon smoked paprika
4 cloves garlic, crushed
1.2kg (42 ounces) canned crushed tomatoes

2 medium tomatoes (300g), chopped finely
½ cup finely chopped fresh coriander
  (cilantro)
2 teaspoons finely grated lime rind
1 clove garlic, crushed, extra
ROASTED CORN SALSA
3 husked corn cobs (750g)
1 small red onion (100g), chopped coarsely
1 medium avocado (250g), chopped coarsely
250g halved cherry tomatoes
2 tablespoons lime juice
¼ cup coarsely chopped fresh coriander
  (cilantro)

1   Preheat oven to 140°C/280°F.
2   Soak chillies in the boiling water in small heatproof bowl 10 minutes. Discard stalks from chillies; reserve chillies and liquid.
3   Using heavy knife, separate ribs. Heat oil in large deep flameproof baking dish on stove top; cook ribs, in batches, until browned all over. Remove from pan.
4   Cook chorizo, onion, capsicums, paprika and garlic in same heated dish, stirring, until onion softens. Return ribs to dish with undrained crushed tomatoes, chillies and reserved liquid. Cover, transfer to oven; cook about 1 hour.
5   Uncover, return to oven; cook about 1½ hours or until ribs are tender.
6   Meanwhile, make roasted corn salsa.
7   Combine chopped tomato, coriander, rind and extra garlic in small bowl. Cover; refrigerate until required.
8   Top ribs with coriander mixture; serve with roasted corn salsa.

ROASTED CORN SALSA Roast corn cobs on heated oiled grill plate (or grill or barbecue) until browned all over. When corn is cool enough to handle, cut kernels from cobs. Combine corn kernels in medium bowl with onion, avocado, tomatoes, juice and coriander.

ITALIAN BRAISED PORK

serves 6
prep + cook time
3¼ hours
nutritional count per serving
32.8g total fat
(10.7g saturated fat);
2525kJ (604 cal);
7.5g carbohydrate;
66.5g protein; 4.6g fibre

Slow cooker: suitable
to the end of step 7.
Pressure cooker: suitable
to the end of step 6.
Suitable to freeze at the
end of step 6.

Serve with slices of warm
italian bread.
Ask your butcher to roll and
tie the pork shoulder for you.

2 tablespoons olive oil
1.5kg (3¼ pound) pork shoulder,
  rolled and tied
2 cloves garlic, crushed
1 medium brown onion (150g),
  chopped coarsely
½ small fennel bulb (100g), chopped coarsely
8 slices hot pancetta (120g), chopped coarsely
1 tablespoon tomato paste
½ cup (125ml) dry white wine
400g (14½ ounces) canned whole tomatoes
1 cup (250ml) chicken stock
1 cup (250ml) water
2 sprigs fresh rosemary
2 large fennel bulbs (1kg), halved, sliced thickly

SPICE RUB
1 teaspoon fennel seeds
2 teaspoons dried oregano
½ teaspoon cayenne pepper
1 tablespoon cracked black pepper
1 tablespoon sea salt
2 teaspoons olive oil

1   Preheat oven to 160°C/325°F.
2   Heat oil in large flameproof casserole dish on stove top; cook pork until browned all over.
3   Meanwhile, combine ingredients for spice rub in small bowl.
4   Remove pork from dish; discard all but 1 tablespoon of the oil in dish. Cook garlic, onion, chopped fennel and pancetta in same heated dish, stirring, until onion softens. Add paste; cook, stirring, 2 minutes.
5   Meanwhile, rub pork with spice rub.
6   Return pork to dish with wine, undrained tomatoes, stock, the water and rosemary; bring to the boil. Cover, transfer to oven; cook 1 hour.
7   Add sliced fennel to dish; cook, covered, in oven 1 hour. Remove pork from dish; discard rind. Cover pork to keep warm.
8   Meanwhile, cook braising liquid in dish over medium heat on stove top, uncovered, until thickened slightly. Return sliced pork to dish; serve pork with sauce.

CHICKPEA VEGETABLE BRAISE WITH CUMIN COUSCOUS

1 cup (200g) dried chickpeas (garbanzo beans)
2 tablespoons olive oil
2 small leeks (400g), chopped coarsely
2 medium carrots (240g), cut into batons
2 cloves garlic, crushed
1 tablespoon finely chopped fresh rosemary
2 tablespoons white wine vinegar
2 cups (500ml) vegetable stock
100g (3 ounces) baby spinach leaves

¼ cup (60ml) lemon juice
2 tablespoons olive oil, extra
2 cloves garlic, crushed, extra
CUMIN COUSCOUS
1 cup (250ml) boiling water
1 cup (200g) couscous
1 tablespoon olive oil
1 teaspoon ground cumin

serves 4
prep + cook time
1¾ hours (+ standing)
nutritional count per serving
26.9g total fat
(3.9g saturated fat);
2483kJ (594 cal);
63.2g carbohydrate;
49g protein; 11.4g fibre

Slow cooker: suitable
to the end of step 3.
Pressure cooker: suitable
to the end of step 1.
Suitable to freeze at the
end of step 3.

1   Place chickpeas in medium bowl, cover with cold water; stand overnight, drain. Rinse under cold water; drain. Place chickpeas in medium saucepan of boiling water; return to the boil. Reduce heat; simmer, uncovered, about 40 minutes or until chickpeas are tender. Drain.
2   Meanwhile, preheat oven to 140°C/280°F.
3   Heat oil in large deep flameproof baking dish on stove top; cook leek and carrot, stirring, until just tender. Add garlic, rosemary and chickpeas; cook, stirring, until fragrant. Add vinegar and stock; bring to the boil. Cover, transfer to oven; cook 30 minutes.
4   Meanwhile, make cumin couscous.
5   Remove dish from oven; stir in spinach, juice, extra oil and extra garlic. Serve with couscous.

CUMIN COUSCOUS Combine the water and couscous in medium heatproof bowl, cover; stand about 5 minutes or until liquid is absorbed, fluffing with fork occasionally. Add oil and cumin; toss gently to combine.

ham hock the lower portion of the leg; includes the meat, fat and bone. Most have been cured, smoked or both.

neck sometimes called pork scotch; a boneless cut from the foreloin.

pancetta an Italian unsmoked bacon; pork belly cured in salt and spices then rolled into a sausage shape and dried for several weeks. Used, sliced or chopped, as an ingredient rather than eaten on its own.

prosciutto cured, unsmoked, pressed ham.

sausage, italian pork available as both sweet, which is flavoured with garlic and fennel seed, and hot, which has chilli.

shoulder joint sold with the bone in or out.

spare ribs (american-style spareribs); well-trimmed mid-loin ribs.

POTATOES, BABY NEW also known as chats; not a separate variety but an early harvest with very thin skin; good, unpeeled and steamed, and eaten, hot or cold, in salads.

PRAWNS also known as shrimp.

PRESERVED LEMON RIND a North African specialty; lemons are quartered and preserved in salt and lemon juice or water. To use, remove and discard pulp, squeeze juice from rind, then rinse rind well and slice thinly. Sold in delicatessens and major supermarkets.

RAISINS dried sweet grapes.

RAS EL HANOUT a classic spice blend used in Moroccan cooking. The name means 'top of the shop' and is the very best spice blend a spice merchant has to offer. Most versions contain over a dozen spices, including cardamom, mace, nutmeg, cinnamon and ground chilli.

RICE
basmati a white, fragrant long-grained rice. Wash several times before cooking.
medium-grain previously sold as calrose rice; an extremely versatile rice that can be substituted for short- or long-grain rices if necessary.

RISONI small, rice-shaped pasta similar to orzo; used in soups and salads.

ROMANO CHEESE a hard, sheep's- or cow's-milk cheese. Straw-coloured and grainy in texture, it's mainly used for grating. Substitute with parmesan.

SAFFRON available in strands (threads) or ground form; imparts a yellow-orange colour to food once infused. Quality varies greatly; the best is the most expensive spice in the world. Should be stored in the freezer.

SAUCES
char siu a Chinese barbecue sauce made from sugar, water, salt, fermented soya bean paste, honey, soy sauce, malt syrup and spices. Found at most supermarkets.

fish also called nam pla or nuoc nam; made from pulverised salted fermented fish, most often anchovies. Has a very pungent smell and strong taste, so use according to your taste level.

oyster Asian in origin, this rich, brown sauce is made from oysters and their brine, cooked with salt and soy sauce, and thickened with starches.

soy also known as sieu, is made from fermented soya beans. Several variations are available in most supermarkets and Asian food stores. We use a mild Japanese variety in our recipes; possibly the best table soy and the one to choose if you only want one variety.

light soy a fairly thin, pale but salty tasting sauce; used in dishes in which the natural colour of the ingredients is to be maintained. Not to be confused with salt-reduced or low-sodium soy sauces.

tamari a thick, dark soy sauce made mainly from soya beans, but without the wheat used in most standard soy sauces.

tomato pasta made from a blend of tomatoes, herbs and spices.

worcestershire a dark-coloured condiment made from garlic, soy sauce, tamarind, onions, molasses, lime, anchovies, vinegar and seasonings.

SAUSAGES minced meat seasoned with salt and spices, mixed with cereal and packed into casings. Also known as snags or bangers.

SILVER BEET also known as swiss chard and mistakenly called spinach; a member of the beet family grown for its tasty green leaves and celery-like stems. Best cooked rather than eaten raw. Also known as blettes.

SOUR CREAM a thick commercially-cultured soured cream. Minimum fat content 35%.

SOURDOUGH has a lightly sour taste from the yeast starter culture used to make the bread. A low-risen dense bread with a crisp crust.

SPLIT PEAS a variety of yellow or green pea grown specifically for drying. When dried, the peas usually split along a natural seam. Whole and split dried peas are available packaged in supermarkets and in bulk in health-food stores.

STAR ANISE dried star-shaped pod having an astringent aniseed flavour; used to favour stocks and marinades. Available whole and ground, it is an essential ingredient in five-spice powder.

SUGAR
caster also known as superfine or finely granulated table sugar.
dark brown a moist, dark brown sugar with a rich, distinctive full flavour coming from natural molasses syrup.
light brown a very soft, finely granulated sugar that retains molasses for its colour and flavour.
white a coarsely granulated table sugar, also known as crystal sugar.

SULTANAS dried grapes that are also known as golden raisins.

TAMARI *see sauces.*

TAMARIND CONCENTRATE the distillation of tamarind pulp into a condensed, compacted paste with a sweet-sour, slightly astringent taste. Thick and purple-black, it requires no soaking. Found in Asian food stores and supermarkets.

TOFU also known as bean curd, an off-white, custard-like product made from the 'milk' of crushed soya beans; comes fresh as soft or firm. Leftover fresh tofu can be refrigerated in water (which is changed daily) for up to four days.
silken tofu refers to the method by which it is made – where it is strained through silk.

TOMATOES
egg also called plum or roma; a smallish, oval-shaped tomato.
paste triple-concentrated tomato puree.
puree canned pureed tomatoes (not tomato paste). Substitute with fresh peeled and pureed tomatoes.

TORTILLAS thin, round unleavened bread originating in Mexico. Two types are available one made from wheat flour, the other from corn.

TURMERIC, GROUND a member of the ginger family, its root is dried and ground, resulting in the rich yellow powder that gives many Indian dishes their characteristic yellow colour. It is intensely pungent in taste, but not hot.

VANILLA EXTRACT made by extracting the flavour from the vanilla bean pod; the pods are soaked, usually in alcohol, to capture its flavour.

VINEGAR
balsamic made from the juice of Trebbiano grapes; it is a deep rich brown colour with a sweet and sour flavour.
white balsamic is a clear and lighter version of balsamic vinegar; has a fresh, sweet, clean taste.
brown malt made from fermented malt and beech shavings.
cider (apple cider) made from fermented apples.
white made from the spirit of cane sugar.
white wine made from a blend of white wines.

WALNUTS a rich, flavourful nut. Should be plump and firm, not shrivelled or soft. Has a high oil content, so store in the fridge. Pecans can be substituted.

WHITE SWEET POTATO is less sweet than kumara; has an earthy flavour. It has a purple flesh beneath its white skin.

YOGURT we use plain yogurt unless otherwise indicated in the recipe.

ZUCCHINI also known as courgette; small green, yellow or white vegetable belonging to the squash family.

CONVERSION CHART

MEASURES

One Australian metric measuring cup holds approximately 250ml; one Australian metric tablespoon holds 20ml; one Australian metric teaspoon holds 5ml.

The difference between one country's measuring cups and another's is within a two- or three-teaspoon variance, and will not affect your cooking results. North America, New Zealand and the United Kingdom use a 15ml tablespoon.

All cup and spoon measurements are level. The most accurate way of measuring dry ingredients is to weigh them. When measuring liquids, use a clear glass or plastic jug with the metric markings.

We use large eggs with an average weight of 60g.

DRY MEASURES

METRIC	IMPERIAL
15g	½oz
30g	1oz
60g	2oz
90g	3oz
125g	4oz (¼lb)
155g	5oz
185g	6oz
220g	7oz
250g	8oz (½lb)
280g	9oz
315g	10oz
345g	11oz
375g	12oz (¾lb)
410g	13oz
440g	14oz
470g	15oz
500g	16oz (1lb)
750g	24oz (1½lb)
1kg	32oz (2lb)

LIQUID MEASURES

METRIC	IMPERIAL
30ml	1 fluid oz
60ml	2 fluid oz
100ml	3 fluid oz
125ml	4 fluid oz
150ml	5 fluid oz (¼ pint)
190ml	6 fluid oz
250ml	8 fluid oz
300ml	10 fluid oz (½ pint)
500ml	16 fluid oz
600ml	20 fluid oz (1 pint)
1000ml (1 litre)	1¾ pints

LENGTH MEASURES

METRIC	IMPERIAL
3mm	⅛in
6mm	¼in
1cm	½in
2cm	¾in
2.5cm	1in
5cm	2in
6cm	2½in
8cm	3in
10cm	4in
13cm	5in
15cm	6in
18cm	7in
20cm	8in
23cm	9in
25cm	10in
28cm	11in
30cm	12in (1ft)

OVEN TEMPERATURES

These oven temperatures are only a guide for conventional ovens. For fan-forced ovens, check the manufacturer's manual.

	°C (CELSIUS)	°F (FAHRENHEIT)	GAS MARK
Very slow	120	250	½
Slow	150	275-300	1-2
Moderately slow	160	325	3
Moderate	180	350-375	4-5
Moderately hot	200	400	6
Hot	220	425-450	7-8
Very hot	240	475	9

INDEX

This book is published in 2011 by Octopus Publishing Group Limited
based on materials licensed to it by ACP Magazines Ltd, a division of PBL Media Pty Limited
54 Park St, Sydney
GPO Box 4088, Sydney, NSW 2001
phone (02) 9282 8618; fax (02) 9267 9438
acpbooks@acpmagazines.com.au; www.acpbooks.com.au

OCTOPUS BOOKS
Published and Distributed in the United Kingdom by Octopus Publishing Group Limited
Endeavour House
189 Shaftesbury Avenue
London WC2H 8JY
United Kingdom
phone + 44 (0) 207 632 5400; fax + 44 (0) 207 632 5405
aww@octopusbooks.co.uk; www.octopusbooks.co.uk
www.australian-womens weekly.com

Printed and bound in China.

International foreign language rights, Brian Cearnes, ACP Books bcearnes@acpmagazines.com.au

A catalogue record for this book is available from the British Library.
ISBN 978-1-90742-823-4

To order Australian Women's Weekly books:
telephone LBS on 01903 828 503
or order online at www.australian-womens-weekly.com
or www.octopusbooks.co.uk

ACP BOOKS
General manager Christine Whiston
Editor-in-chief Susan Tomnay
Creative director & designer Hieu Chi Nguyen
Cover designer Hannah Blackmore
Senior editor Wendy Bryant
Food director Pamela Clark
Food writer Xanthe Roberts
Nutritional information Jordanna Levin
Photographer Ian Wallace
Additional photography John Laurie; David Hahn
Stylist Louise Pickford
Additional styling Simon Bajada
Food preparation Rebecca Squadrito
Additional food preparation Briony Bennett
Sales & rights director Brian Cearnes
Marketing manager Bridget Cody
Senior business analyst Rebecca Varela
Operations manager David Scotto
Production manager Victoria Jefferys

Cover Chicken, lentil and pumpkin curry, page 95
Photographer Ian Wallace
Stylist Louise Pickford
Food preparation Rebecca Squadrito